Hike With Smoky Joe On The Unforgettable Appalachian Trail

This book is a collection of articles in *The Douglas Enterprise*. The first article appeared March 2, 2005. The series, presented in its entirety in this book, was published in 45 parts in the newspaper, the final part appearing on March 22, 2006.

ISBN-13: 978-0-9842626-7-0
ISBN-10: 0-9842626-7-9

First printing, November 2010.

Cover design by Julian Williams & ThomasMax.

Published by:

 tm

ThomasMax Publishing
P.O. Box 250054
Atlanta, GA 30325
404-794-6588
www.thomasmax.com

Hike With Smoky Joe On The Unforgettable Appalachian Trail

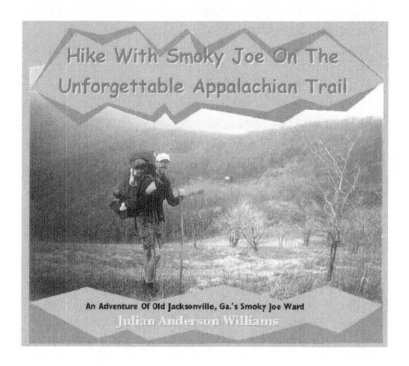

An Adventure Of Old Jacksonville, Ga.'s Smoky Joe Ward
Julian Anderson Williams

Julian Anderson Williams

ThomasMax

Your Publisher
For The 21st Century

Table of Contents

Foreword

Jacksonville, Georgia, is a town of no great physical proportions; the population has shrunk from a post-Revolutionary period and antebellum times of perhaps 500 maximum to a meager 118 in the 21st century. When folks started populating Telfair County around Jacksonville Thomas Jefferson was President. When nearby Fort Clark fought Indians and the town chartered (1815) President James Madison was at the helm. From a stone's throw General John Clark had a plantation and a home. He gave the land ("about an acre") for the church which would become Blockhouse Baptist Church. He would leave there for Milledgeville and become the Governor of Georgia. General Andrew Jackson and Governor John Clark helped and supported General John Coffee (with friend Thomas Swain) as they built the Coffee Road, a military passageway connecting Jacksonville, Georgia, with Tallahassee, Florida.

But, even considering the importance of the location, Jacksonville still scraped for identity, niche and the comforts of life. This status continues to this day. For example, back 65 years ago, some Jacksonville men helped young men appreciate the Boy Scouts experience. But, by the time Smoky Joe Ward, in his youth, was ready for the Boy Scouts experience the privilege had evaporated. So, like many Jacksonville people, Smoky Joe Ward struck out on his own, or with a few friends, to gain an outdoors event. In his case, it was challenging the Appalachian Trail.

Thus, Smoky Joe Ward, as an individual, represents the spirit of Jacksonville, Georgia. No one is expecting some crowd to jump up and join every notion, idea and manifestation of any given subject. Like it or not, a Jacksonvillian is often left alone, with God, to make things work out. But, the situation works out pretty good. The person knows from the beginning he/she cannot blame his/her colleagues for failure or worry about shareholders. In this context, it is a good and necessary plan to include prayer to begin with; but, there is also a time for action. We are reminded by Moses, Exodus 14:15, to then, "Quit praying and get the people moving! Forward, march!" We cannot use prayer as an excuse for not doing anything! I think God would like for us to help a little bit! At least enough to let Him know we are interested in what He is doing! Also, in Jacksonville, like a Georgia sage said, "We don't have anything; but, we have everything." In that frame, Joe Ward was ready to proceed.

In this book, you will see the solid determination of Smoky Joe. You will see his aloneness, without physical companions, but very much close to God. You will see the impact and result of being raised in Jacksonville, Georgia. You will see a man brought down to the barest essentials but endures because he believes. You will see a man who is better because of this experience.

I hope you enjoy the book. Like a previous book, I will use any sales of the book for the Old Jacksonville, Georgia, History Project. We invite you to visit Old Jacksonville, Georgia, and read the history signs erected next to the main (441) highway. When available, I will be happy to do presentations for your group and assist you in any way. Again, thanks for reading this book and contributing to this worthwhile effort. P.S. Also go to Google.com and type in Old Jacksonville, Ga., Photo/Gallery. You will enjoy the pictures and the history.

ABOUT THE AUTHOR

Julian Williams was born June 13, 1940, at Douglas, Ga., and was raised and lived at Jacksonville, Ga. Julian worked with his father at his grocery store and also fished for catfish on the trotlines on the Ocmulgee, Oconee and Altamaha rivers, making a little extra money during the summers.

Julian's elementary and high school grades were primarily spent at Workmore School near Jacksonville, Ga., and Broxton High School in Coffee County. During his U.S. Navy service he enjoyed his work as a Navy Journalist. Later, Julian agreed to accept a temporary teacher position at Broxton High School but the tenure was extended - probably because he could coach the girls' basketball team as he had played the sport at that same school. This teaching experience led to principalships in the Coffee County Schools. He retired from the system after more than 18 years as the Assistant Superintendent of Schools. After completing his postgraduate requirements at Nova University he was named Adjunct Faculty for the Nova Ed.D. Educational Leadership Program for more than 17 years.

Julian has hobbies of reading and writing -- completing more than 500 articles on "The Articles of Old Jacksonville, Ga." He also does sketches, commemorative picture plates and local and historical postcards. He also has many historical and local photographs and images on The Old Jacksonville, Ga., Gallery (PBASE). The gallery can be accessed via Google.com.

Julian's wife, Joanne, is a retired kindergarten teacher. Julian and Joanne have two children, Allison, an RN, and Tara, Pharmacist. They are also proud of their grandchildren: Kate, Abbie, Natalie and Carson.

Julian's first book was published in 2009 – *We Enjoyed Alaska – But Russell Just About Killed Us!* This current book, going to print in 2010, is about the interesting and exciting Appalachian Trail hike of Smoky Joe Ward – *Hike With Smoky Joe On The Unforgettable Appalachian Trail.* Also, look for Julian's third book coming in 2011.

Julian can be reached via email at williamsjulian@hotmail.com or by telephone at 912-384-7178.

*I dedicate this book to Smoky Joe Ward and his family who have meant so much to me and others –
his father, Rev. Wade, Mrs. Helen, his mother and Rev. Murray, his brother.*

Also, to John David Harrell, who stuck with Smoky Joe through it all and was his trip support man and trail coordinator.

Part 1
Thoughts About Attempting The Appalachian Trail Hike

Joe Ward, left, and John David Harrell, right, talk over details concerning the hiking of The Appalachian Trail. The Trail extends from Georgia to Maine and is 2,160 miles of challenge. Joe Ward of Jacksonville, Ga., decided to hike the entire Trail. Did he make it? Join us on The Trail with Joe to see what he faced and how he fared.

Most of us take "walks" from time to time. We usually have comfortable shoes on our feet, a nice flat terrain, good weather and we usually walk a mile or two. Maybe a little more or a little less. Sometimes we even walk on an inside track. We call it "exercise" and the practice of this ritual helps our consciences a lot and our bodies a little bit. If we can produce a little perspiration we feel even better about the ordeal. Your sweaty shirt becomes your badge of honor. You did not cheat the system. But, all that hogwash sort of goes out the window when we look at the accomplishment of an Appalachian Trail hiker.

In fact, it is difficult for me to visualize the feat of Joe Ward of Jacksonville, Ga. He walked the entire length of the Appalachian Trail from Georgia to Maine -- 2,160 miles. In miles that would be about eleven trips on foot from Douglas, Ga., to Athens, Ga. But even that comparison will not suffice to let us know what Joe accomplished. To get a little sense of the rigor required I would suggest you go up to North Carolina and walk up one of those little mountains. Your legs will begin to get the idea that you have just engaged in a new kind of walking. You will begin to see what a challenge Joe Ward had accepted when he decided to conquer the Appalachian Trail. I believe that is better terminology than "to walk the Appalachian Trail."

Why did Joe challenge The Trail? Folks do it for different reasons. I would have had to exhaust all other avenues of sustaining life and limb - The Trail being my only option for survival. And I mean ONLY. I would have hunted many roads and avenues of escape before confronting The Trail.

But Joe Ward had hiking in his genes. His father was Rev. Wade Ward, a peripatetic Baptist preacher if ever there was one. That means he walked a lot. He walked for the joy of it. He walked for the exercise. He walked while preparing his sermons. He walked to get away from the rest of us. He just walked and walked and walked. The woods around Jacksonville, Ga., are full of the sermons he composed. We called our preacher "Brother Ward." I think Brother Ward felt closer to Nature and his Maker out there. I would like to know the total number of miles he walked.

Joe is a lot like his daddy. He enjoys the freedom of that world that exists apart from the one we usually awake to each morning. This was a chance to relieve the stress and molding of the routine ruts of his life. This was a once-in-a-lifetime opportunity. This was "the way he needed to go" at that point in his life.

It all began back around 1983. My first cousin, John David Harrell, had an active part in the process that led to Joe's Appalachian Trail endeavor. John related to me that he and a friend, Bob Walker, accompanied high school students to the mountains to hike. At the time John and Bob did not think about hiking much themselves as they were busy setting up camp, giving guidance and supervision and "looking after" the students.

But John and Bob began to talk. The hiking bug had bitten them. Soon they called two other friends. Four young men were soon on the way to the starting point of the Appalachian Trail - John David Harrell, Bob Walker, Will Hope and Joe Ward. Bob Walker, with military experience, became the leader of the pack. He began to show the others the ropes of hiking. During this same time they began to gather equipment. Soon they were ready.

When they arrived at their departure point near Amicalola Falls in North Georgia they were still a little ways, and a rough little ways, from The Trail.   But Bob knew a "short cut." Right up the side of the mountain! So up they went but soon tired and had to quit and camp and didn't make it to The Trail that day. But they finally made it to The Trail and enjoyed hiking portions of it. They were getting their feet wet. And enjoyed it. They repeated their visits to The Trail several times. It was becoming like a magnet - a part of them not to be denied. The Trail had something they needed. They looked forward to this communion. It was turning into a dedicated effort. And then it turned into something else. Obsession.

The Trail became a must. An imperative. They had to tackle it. It was something that could not be ignored. Their feelings must have been similar to those of our three-year-old granddaughter, Abbie. When we ask her why she did something, she replies, "I had to." They "had to" engage The Trail.

Now the group was reduced to Joe Ward and John David Harrell. Together they decided to do all the Georgia section of The Trail. The logistics and strategies of taking on The Trail are not that simple. Food packages must arrive by mail at certain places at certain times. Hiking times and distances must be calculated to coincide with the arrival of those packages. Many other preparations had to be made. But it was a start. It was the beginning of the conquest of The Trail.

Here some of the young men (students on the trip) take a break. These youngsters found what The Trail was all about. Who knows? Some day they might hike the Appalachian Trail!

Bob Walker   Joe Ward   John Harrell   David   Will Hope

These young ladies of the student body also wanted to learn hiking skills. It looks like they are ready to go hiking. And you won't learn these experiences from a book. Now they will see if they are in shape.

Credits: Info of Joe Ward; Info of John David Harrell; personal notes; other sources.

Part 2
Large And Small Animals Could Eat Your Lunch!

Photo Credit:
David Kirshner & Frank Knight

Joe Ward and John David Harrell of Jacksonville, Ga., fell in love with the Appalachian Trail. Whether they loved those black bears they encountered might be another matter. The black bear was only one of the "critters" they met on The Trail. The Appalachian Trail was a good teacher and worthy challenge.

Joe Ward and John David Harrell, after several trips to the mountains, were getting attached to the idea of hiking the Appalachian Trail. They finally got to the point of wanting to see if their yearnings were valid urges of the will or just idle daydreams. For a test they decided to try a ten-day trip to cover the Georgia section of the Appalachian Trail. These Jacksonville, Ga., natives were about to test some waters they had never waded in.

The day for undertaking the Georgia section of The Trail arrived. Joe and John stopped at Amicalola Falls and left their truck. Joe's mother, Mrs. Helen Ward, and an aunt transported Joe and John from

Amicalola to the Georgia-North Carolina border. There the young men were left. They had to hike back to Amicalola or get there some way. Joe's mother and aunt wished the fellows luck, waved goodbye and returned to Jacksonville, Ga.

Joe and John would be hiking north to south. Although they would only be doing the Georgia section of The Trail this is the way many hike the entire Appalachian Trail. They start in Maine and walk to Georgia. Others reverse the hike and begin in Georgia.

Joe and John knew they would learn valuable lessons on The Trail as they headed back into Georgia from North Carolina. Lesson Number One was soon coming. Lesson One: They had too much in their packs. Starting out they didn't seem so heavy. After a while their packs seemed to weigh more and more. As they hiked they noticed discarded items along The Trail. Other hikers had discarded their extra stuff along The Trail. They knew from that experience they had to figure out how to reduce the content of their packs. They had to get as light as possible but retain enough to get by on.

For the first couple of days Joe and John didn't make much time but as they got used to The Trail they began to pick up speed. Relatively speaking of course. The Appalachian Trail is not the Indianapolis Speedway. More like the difference in a turtle walking and one running.

They also tested the logistics of their food supplies. To get their mailed food packets they had to walk into town. Once they left The Trail and walked into Suches. Another town that was a welcome sight for sore eyes and feet was Helen, Ga. The Bavaria Alpine atmosphere of the mountain village was a welcome relief from the rigors of mountain hiking. There they cooled their heels and partook of the expected food. A fellow could get used to the comfort of Helen, Ga. But Helen was not where the challenge was. They had to return to The Trail.

Lesson Two had been learned. Get a little food and comfort and get back to business. They headed back to The Trail and hiked separately so each could establish his "own gait" and not impede the progress of the other.

With this arrangement of separation John was ahead of Joe on The Trail. As John progressed along the path he came upon his first surprise: a black bear in the middle of The Trail! Now, let's figure here a little. John had just had lunch and didn't need any food at the time. Question: Had the black bear had lunch and, if hungry, what would he eat? John hoped he himself would not become a candidate for bear food! But before John could get closer, or farther away, the black bear made a fast exit. Still concerned, John wrote Joe a note in the dirt: "Watch for bear!" Believe it or not, when Joe came along later he saw the message scratched in the path of The Trail. But they never saw the bear again - at least not that one.

Lesson Three: There are more creatures than just you out there on The Appalachian Trail. Be ready to encounter a variety of them at any time. Now, that in itself would probably create in me some anxiety about my chances of hiking the Appalachian Trail. Oh, some say, that's just an old black bear. Not a grizzly. Well, I am by bears like I am about snakes. A bear is a bear and it might have little ones around. And I can think of a lot of places I'd rather be than in close communion with a bear on the Appalachian Trail. Any kind of bear. There is just not room enough for both of us there at the same place and same time!

Lesson Four coming up. Related to Number Three above because it also involves more of those creatures on The Trail. But the difference was the size of the creature. This latest lesson was taught by a smaller critter - a small mouse.

As Joe and John found the trail shelters they were delighted they had a place to hang their hats for a while and relax. Here they could pull their heavy packs off and rest a spell. Then they could doze off in peaceful sleep and pleasant dreams. Or so they thought.

As they slept the small mice critters were hard at work - chewing holes in their packs to get their food. Upon awaking Joe and John could not believe their eyes. All those holes gnawed in their packs.

From then on they would prefer sleeping in their tents. The bears might get them but they would be out of those mice-infested shelters. The lessons were piling up. But they were learning fast. The Appalachian Trail was a good teacher and would be a worthy challenge.

Credits: Info of Joe Ward; Info of John David Harrell; personal notes; other sources.

Part 3
Testing The Challenge – Hiking The Georgia Section Of The Trail

Joe Ward, center, is flanked by his Aunt Lula Lawhorne, left, and his mother, Helen Ward, right. These ladies gave Joe Ward and John David Harrell a ride to the North Carolina line. After saying their "goodbyes" the ladies returned to Jacksonville, Ga., and the young men began their adventure of hiking the Georgia section of the Appalachian Trail. They found The Trail to be a great challenge and a great teacher. [Photo credit: John David Harrell]

In a way it seemed like a long time ago to Joe Ward and John David Harrell when Joe's mother, Mrs. Helen Ward, and his aunt, Mrs. Lula Lawhorne, dropped them off at the North Carolina line. The ladies waved goodbye and the young men started their hike back to

Georgia along the Appalachian Trail. Mrs. Ward and Mrs. Lawhorne were soon back at Jacksonville, Ga., safe and dry. But it was not so with the fellows on The Trail.

Descending down into Georgia on the Appalachian Trail is probably not a good way of describing climbing mountains. Whether you are going north or south on The Trail there are mountains to climb. Joe Ward and John David Harrell were engaged in a ten-day ordeal of hiking from the North Carolina line down to the starting point of the Appalachian Trail in Georgia. They wanted to get a good tasty sampling of what it would be like to hike the entire Trail.

And they were getting a very good sample indeed. They were about in the middle of their journey in the last week of August, 1983, when they encountered one day of rain. They suited up in their rain gear - pants and jackets. But they were not out of the woods with the rain. The sultry heat began to combine with the rain to make an uncomfortable situation for the young men from Jacksonville, Georgia. Their outfits were becoming steam capsules and now their clothes were soaking wet on the inside! So things weren't going well inside or out!

Trudging through the steady rain Neels Gap looked like a haven of rest. And it was because there was a store, shelter and other facilities there. When Joe and John arrived there they were miserable. They couldn't wait to clean up and get dry clothes.

Luckily the man who ran the store at Neels Gap had a wife who worked at the nearby park run by the Department of Natural Resources. Being able to use the washer and dryer there was a pleasant surprise. After they got themselves and their clothing clean and dry the man at the store allowed them to sleep in the store's restroom overnight. Although it had a concrete floor they inflated their ever-present air mattresses and had a decent place to rest for the night. Things were really looking up.

Waking in the morning they were eager to leave the restroom to those who needed it for other purposes. Although they had stayed up and talked a good bit the night before they were rested and eager to continue their journey. The shining sun and the singing birds welcomed Joe and John to a new day on The Trail. Things were still looking up.

The opening of the store was their signal to vacate the restroom. And they were eternally grateful for that restroom. They were also grateful to the man for letting them use it for sleeping quarters. They chatted with him a while and purchased some items of clothing from him before continuing down The Trail. But "down" meant "up" for a steep mountain lay ahead.

We emphasize the word "up" because their next challenge on The Trail would be Blood Mountain. Blood Mountain has a somewhat sanguinary sounding name and if we look into history a little we will see why. It seems the Creek Indians wanted to extend their territory a bit up that way but found the Cherokees quite unwilling to relinquish their mountainous real estate.:

Thus, the 4,458-foot peak became the site of a fierce battle between those two native American groups. The view from up there is incredible but the Indians were so busy killing each other they probably didn't have time to admire the scenery from the overlook.

"According to the legend so many warriors died in the battle that their blood ran down the sides of the mountain and into the rivers turning everything red. It is easy to see from that legend alone how the mountain got its unique name. The Cherokee also thought that Blood Mountain was home to the Nunnehi. The Nunnehi were a spirit people that watched over hunters and people hiking through the region."

As we said, the view from up there on Blood Mountain is incredible, but like the Indians, Joe and John didn't get a chance to admire the scenery either. A dense fog had set in - maybe from that previous rain and humidity. They couldn't even take pictures for the fog. Denied the great views from that lofty pinnacle named Blood Mountain they probably were content to get a rest from the steep ascent they had just made. They didn't mention seeing any Nunnehi spirit people. And probably glad they didn't. But Joe and John were certainly glad to be there anyway. It wouldn't be long before they reached their goal - the end of The Trail in Georgia.

Descending Blood Mountain they turned their eager gazes south.

Joe and John met many challenges and learned a lot on The Trail and we will talk about some of those things as we continue. The Trail was a great challenge and a great teacher.

P.S. Smoky Joe's father would have liked to have been there hiking with Smoky Joe. Below is picture of his daddy (No. 5).

Jacksonville Lions Club

We include this picture because Smoky Joe's father, Rev. Wade Ward, is in the picture (No. 5); he was a very good friend of my father, J.D. Williams (No. 7). Pictured are: John David Harrell (No. 1), Joe's coordinator on The Trail, Charles Jones (No. 2), Leon Wilkes (No. 3), Eschol Knight (No. 4), Rev. Wade Ward (No. 5), Waverly Larkey (No. 6), J.D. Williams (No. 7), Frank Ray, Jr. (8), Preston Fussell (No. 9), Earl Bland (No. 10), Walter Wells (No. 11), Frank Ray, Sr. (No. 12), Guy Bland (No. 13), J.Q. Russ (No. 14) and Emory Jones (No. 15). This picture of the Jacksonville, Ga., Lions was taken c. 1978 at the Jacksonville Lions Clubhouse.

Credits: Info of Joe Ward; Info of John David Harrell; "Blood Mountain" by David Cook; Image of the Jacksonville Lions Club with Rev. Wade Ward (Smoky Joe's father); personal notes; other sources.

Part 4
You Have To Watch What You Eat And Drink

John David Harrell, left, and Joe Ward, right, warmed up to the task of hiking the Appalachian Trail by hiking the 100 miles of the Georgia section of The Trail. These Jacksonville, Ga., natives found some interesting things on the Appalachian Trail. The little fellow in the center is our new grandson, Joseph Carson Neeley, who may one day hike the Appalachian Trail. If he doesn't do that maybe he will find another worthwhile challenge. [Photo credit: John David Harrell]

Right away you will notice that I have unprofessionally included a picture of our newborn grandson in the Appalachian Trail picture that accompanies this article. I did this for several reasons: (1) I wanted everyone to see our new grandson, Joseph Carson Neeley. (2) Since he shares the name Joseph with Joe Ward, our Jacksonville, Ga., hiker, we hope that he, like Joe, will one day want to hike the Appalachian Trail. (3) He will be called Carson, not Joe, and hopefully he will find, if not the Appalachian Trail, some kind of challenge that he can convert into a contribution to life.

When we sent out a picture of the nine pounds, one ounce boy we immediately got two replies from interested persons wanting to know if the University of Georgia football recruiters had shown up at the hospital. They could already envision his 21-inch frame being potentially extended into the red and black uniform of a Bulldog linebacker.

So, maybe one day Carson Neeley will hike the Appalachian Trail and can again be in the picture with Joe Ward and John David Harrell. Whether he can take The Trail remains to be seen for according to John Harrell there are some inconveniences out there on that trying path that leads from Georgia to Maine.

For instance, we take water for granted. Out on The Trail water is a necessity just as it is with us back home. One can get into trouble drinking water from holes and streams. John told me the safest drinking water was found flowing out of a rock or the side of a mountain. That water is usually pure and untainted. Getting a stomach full of bad water could cause problems you don't want or need.

Another thing to look for on The Trail is the weather. The weather can suddenly change. It might be pleasant down on the "flatlands" but as soon as you get up there on The Trail you can encounter very windy conditions, extreme cold and misting rain. You have to be ready for these opposing weather conditions of "two worlds." This one down here and that one up there in the sky.

As Joe and John hiked the Georgia portion of The Trail they also experienced what it was like to come up with a meal. Not many restaurants are out there on the Appalachian Trail but surprisingly there are some restaurants in some of the towns not far off The Trail and it was always a treat to be able to partake of great portions of that seldom-found food.

Usually though, the eating fare was not very sensational at all. John said he and Joe carried a small gas stove with them with small containers of fuel. They also had rice in little plastic bags - Success Rice - and this staple was a favorite food on The Trail. It was also fairly simple to prepare. You boil it in an aluminum pot, it puffs up in the bag and presto! - your meal is done. They also, for the sake of variety, had something called Ala Carte, a mixture of precooked meat and vegetables. Carson, our new grandson, could probably eat that and a lot more. He seems to be eating about everything they offer him at the hospital. Carson came by C-Section early. They said he probably would have weighed twelve pounds if he had gone full term. Probably been about ready at that point to hike the Appalachian Trail!

But the ability to hike the Appalachian Trail is not the only attribute a hiker needs to have. Being a good steward of The Trail is so important to the reputation and character of the hiker, to others on The

Trail and to The Trail itself. Products made of paper or cardboard are most desirable. These products can be buried or burned and they "go back to the earth." Plastics are a no-no and plastics and metals are usually kept in one's pack until they can be properly disposed of at a store or disposal station. If the Appalachian Trail looked like some of our highway rights-of-way it would be a sight that would make your eyes sore! Fortunately, most Trail hikers are nature people and want to see Nature at its best. They also want to protect this great treasure.

As I considered all these things to be considered by a hiker I asked John what would be "a good day of hiking?" John replied that a good day would be making twelve miles or more. He said a bad day would be five to six miles, if that.

Think about it. From Georgia to Maine - 2,160 miles of near deprivation, some starvation or getting mighty hungry for some good vittles, encountering all sorts of weather and trying to make those tired and aching feet go one more mile. And then another. And another. And at the same time looking for those bears and snakes!

And speaking of snakes we will tell you a snake story as we continue on our travels along the Appalachian Trail. It won't be long before Carson Neeley, our grandson, will be into such things as hiking The Appalachian Trail. I would like to see the faces of his parents when they get the word he is "hiking The Trail." Good luck, Carson.

Credits: Info of Joe Ward; Info of John David Harrell; personal notes; other sources.

Part 5
Make Sure You Look Under The Rocks!

John David Harrell, left, and Joe Ward, right, of Jacksonville, Ga., stand beside the "Deep Gap" sign near the North Carolina line where they set out hiking the Georgia section of the Appalachian Trail. It took them ten days and they had some learning experiences. Enough to encourage Joe Ward to later hike the entire Appalachian Trail - approximately 2,160 miles. [Photo credit: John David Harrell]

Joe Ward and John David Harrell continued their long walk on the Appalachian Trail. They were now making great progress in completing their goal. Their goal was to hike the Georgia section of the The Trail. They had started their trip near the North Carolina border and now that was far behind them and Springer Mountain and their truck at Amicalola Falls were becoming realities not far away. It would be good to see that truck.

After almost dismissing the first meeting with a black bear, they were about content to forgo "bear watching" but other surprises awaited them. One day found them on the top of a majestic mountain; they could see far into the beautiful and awesome distance. God had indeed provided some grand scenery up there. To add to the awe-inspiring atmosphere lightning flashed around the tops of trees on distant peaks. It was a sight to behold. To really absorb the moment the young men quickly found a fine seat - the big smooth top of a flat rock - just the place to sit and survey the wonder being exhibited before them. It just didn't get much better than this.

But the solemnity and serenity of the moment was interrupted by a sound that ran chills up the spine of Joe Ward. He grabbed the arm of John Harrell and excitedly said, "Get out of here!"

Now what they had seen was a fine big flat rock to sit on. What they had not seen was the rattlesnake that rested beneath it. I asked John if they tried to get the snake out from underneath "their" rock. He told me they didn't try very hard. I said the snake was probably one of those little pygmy rattlers or a timber rattler or something similar. I don't know for sure if those are the mountain type rattlers but I don't think they have those old South Georgia diamond-backs up that far. I suppose they have sidewinders out West. But John was in no mood to try to ferret the snake out of his lair and determine his nomenclature. John summed up the event by saying if that snake would just stay where he was then he and Joe would try to find themselves elsewhere. I believe that was a wise line of thinking.

From the description of bath-taking I assumed that the fellows didn't take many baths during their foray into the wilderness. John said out on The Trail the only bath you could take was the one in a mountain stream. Now, taking a bath out there in the nowhere was an experience in itself. First you had to find a stream deep enough to submerse the extremities you wished washed. Next, was getting up the courage to take the plunge. If you have ever been around mountain stream water you know what I mean. It is like ice water. Grin and bear it. Shaving with ice water is fun, too. Needless to say, it didn't take the fellows long to take a bath and shave. It seemed like John shivered a little just talking about it.

Another experience John said was interesting was meeting various types of people on The Trail. Sometimes they would meet a person with a dog. Other times they might meet a lone female on The Trail. They talked to one of the girls but she said she was comfortable with her situation. Sometimes two people would be hiking together. Many times it would just be one person. I think they saw some who resembled Big Foot. I imagine a person could get pretty ugly if he stayed out there in the wilderness for awhile without the amenities of what we call civilization.

There have been stories of people being killed on The Trail. Sometimes they would get lost and perish. But other times they were victims of their own species - man. We have to acknowledge the fact that there are some crazies out there and some of them have apparently appeared and done malice, at times anyway, on The Trail.

Less damaging, but not pleasant either, were attacks by yellow jackets. The little pests will build nest in rocks right under the surface of the ground and if you happen to disturb one of these habitats you will have a fight with the yellow jackets. And they usually win.

Well, this time around Joe and John dodged the bear, the snake, human assailants, and the yellow jacket. They avoided the mice with all their infestations and diseases and altogether put together a pretty safe trip. Whether they wanted to tackle a larger piece of The Trail remained to be seen. This was enough for right now.

Thankful for all that happened to them and equally thankful for all that did not, the fellows arrived at Springer Mountain on the ninth day and made Amicalola Falls on the tenth day. That truck was looking better all the time.

On the last night it was cold enough to build a campfire. Sitting around the fire Joe and John had an opportunity to assess their experience. It had been a good one.

On the approach to Amicalola they ran into some girls who asked where they had been. They proudly answered that they had been hiking The Trail for ten days. Walking away, the girls, thinking they were beyond the ears of Joe and John, said, "They sure smell like they have been on The Trail for ten days!"

But they had already resolved to settle that - first thing - a good shower! And then they headed home. But there would be other days on the Appalachian Trail - all of it!

Credits: Info of Joe Ward; Info of John David Harrell; personal notes; other sources.

Part 6
Making The Big Decision

Joe Ward and John David Harrell of Jacksonville, Ga., met many interesting people on the Georgia section of the Appalachian Trail. Two of those folks are pictured here. Sorry but we don't have their names. Sixteen years after this hike Joe decided to tackle the entire Trail from Georgia to Maine. John remained as his support person at home base. He had suffered broken legs in his duties as a volunteer fireman. Joe was about to meet some more interesting folks. [Photo credit: John David Harrell]

Joe Ward and John David Harrell had now finished the Georgia section of the Appalachian Trail. Their walk in the wilderness up there in the northern part of our state had afforded the young men from Jacksonville, Ga., a view of what it was like to walk in the wild. After a long hot shower they were now clean enough to get close enough to regular citizens without having to address them from downwind. But they were not interested in interviews at this point with folks who couldn't stand a little trail musk. They wanted to crank up that truck and go home. Loving kin and friends awaited their arrival.

Fortunately, they came home with no spotted ticks attached to critical areas of their bodies. They also were devoid of the countless maladies available through the mice-infested hiking trail shelters they tried so hard to adroitly avoid. There was a feeling of unlimited satisfaction in knowing they had befuddled those little microscopic sarcoptic parasites that cause such things as mange or scabies. No itchy onset of head lice. The few initial mites they had close communion with had long since departed their bodies. Their cool foreheads showed no signs of undulant fever and they figured the ground squirrel walking sideways did not have rabies after all. Probably just drunk on the wrong kind of wild berries. They bore no gunshot wounds from crazy hikers or ambushers along The Trail and of course, as we previously mentioned, the two deftly sidestepped the noisy rattlesnake which primed itself beneath the large smooth rock they were sitting on. He abruptly interrupted their attempt to admire one especially beautiful lightning-enhanced majestic mountain horizon. So much for over-whelming scenery.

To some the avoidance of these myriad medical inconveniences and wilderness hazards seems of little consequence. But if these critics were out there with lightning flashing, water filling up their tents, and some unknown banshee, or imitating critter, wailing out a scream of possible death or worse, then they might reconsider their criticisms.

But Joe and John learned a lot. The Trail was a good teacher and the young men would remember their lessons.

Sixteen years passed by - from 1983 to 1999 - and Joe and John toyed with the idea of tackling the entire Appalachian Trail. Neither was getting any younger. Off and on they would toy with various parts of The Trail. They went just often enough to whet their suppressed desire to hike the entire Trail from Georgia to Maine.

But fate was to deal a blow to John Harrell which would keep him from hiking The Trail with Joe Ward. In responding to a fire call, John, a Jacksonville, Ga., volunteer fireman, fell from the fire truck and broke both legs. His role in conquering the Appalachian Trail had changed. But he did not give up the dream of The Trail. If Joe would do it he would help him from home base. He would be his support person.

But Joe was wrestling with the question of walking The Trail. It seemed like walking was in his legs. His father, Rev. Wade Ward, had probably walked the total miles of the circumference of the Earth in the many years he tirelessly strode over the hills and through the gullies of

Jacksonville, Ga. He walked the streets, the pastures, the piney woods, the sandy oak knolls, the river swamp - anywhere Nature provided. He was a walker if ever there was one. And Joe told me, "No doubt Dad had a great influence on me. Early in my life we would take our vacations up around Helen, Ga., and walk those mountain trails and other places. I had no idea at the time the place was near The Appalachian Trail. In fact, at that time, I knew nothing of The Trail. I had never heard of it."

But Joe practiced walking on the swamp roads of the wildlife management area between Jacksonville, Ga., and Lumber City. Down there near Scuffle Bluff and Montgomery Lake (home of the World Record Largemouth Bass) and Staves Landing. Down there where a fellow can walk and sort through things. I assume Joe walked all that by the light of day. I know from personal experience a fellow can get lost down there at night.

So Joe walked and walked some more and mused upon that exhilarating challenge of the wild blue yonder - that long stretch of mountains from Georgia to Maine - known as The Appalachian Trail.

One day he went to his friend John Harrell and said, "John I want to ask you something and I want you to tell me not to do it. I want to walk The Appalachian Trail."

John grinned at Joe and that grin reflected the pride of both men. It reflected the dream they both had. It reflected that a job they had started now had a great possibility of being finished. It reflected more than words can describe.

John looked at his friend and said, "Joe, I am not going to tell you not to do it. I am going to tell you to do it. Go for it. You can do it."

That night was a sleepless one for Joe Ward - and John David Harrell. Much planning had to be done. Joe had not really done much research at this point. But he had ordered a few trail guides and had some information.

Joe and John had met some interesting folks on the Georgia section. Joe could just imagine the folks he would encounter as he tried to walk from Georgia to Maine. And the critters and all the other things.

Credits: Info of Joe Ward; Info of John David Harrell; personal notes; other sources.

Part 7
Starting The Appalachian Trail

Joe Ward started out on the Appalachian Trail and the rain was coming down. The next day the rain had slackened and he found himself at Woody Gap, an isolated place near Suches, Ga. Even Woody Gap School is an "isolated school." But the people there make wise use of their resources. Joe Ward had to do the same as he hiked the Appalachian Trail. [Photo credit: Woody Gap School]

Even starting the Appalachian Trail is a chore. Joe Ward and John David Harrell of Jacksonville, Ga., had their last supper together and it was trout. It was nice to see the browned and tasty fish in front of you ready for eating. Joe Ward would find some of his other meals on the Appalachian Trail harder to come by. And not near as tasty.

Joe eyed the comfortable and dry surroundings of the lodge at Amicalola. He knew it would not be like this on The Trail. Against this background of comfort and serenity he was reminded of the wilderness by the sound of the falling water of nearby Amicalola Falls. The night did not obscure the power of the 729 foot-high falls as the crystal-clear waters cascaded down the levels hewn by thousands of years of activity. The Cherokees had named these falling waters appropriately - "tumbling waters."

Between the lodge and the falls Joe would find the beginning of the Southern Terminus Trail. Stone steps rising from the lodge road would put one on this terminus access trail. This trail would lead to Springer Mountain, the official starting point of the Appalachian Trail. So Joe would have to walk some eight miles before he was at the starting point of the AT. But John came to his rescue and drove him to about a mile of the beginning of The Trail on Springer Mountain.

"Johnny drove me to base of Springer Mt. on USFS 42 about one mile north of beginning of trail. It was raining when I left him to start trip. I hated to see him drive off. I wasn't well prepared for rain with poncho and old rain pants. Would change later. Walked one mile south to southern terminal of A.T. on Springer Mt. It was raining and so foggy that I didn't sign the register. I began the trip north and camped at Hightower Gap. 8.2 miles."

As related, near Springer Mountain, the two friends parted ways. If they weren't crying they probably felt like it. Now, people are different. I am afraid that my narrative would have been vastly different from the one recorded above for Joe Ward. I don't think I would have gotten out of the truck and walked into a rainy foggy wilderness. I would probably have told John to head the truck south - and step on it! With me in it!

Even with the rain in his face, Joe thought of "all that out there" in front of him. He mentally sifted through the mountains of information made available to him. Of course, he had not processed all of it but he had to wonder how the rare presence of the eastern milk snake, the pileated woodpecker and the pink lady slipper plant would help or hinder him with the challenge ahead. With this thought Joe grinned because he figured it was raining on them, too.

But you can't ignore your information. From his and John's experience on the Georgia section of The Trail Joe knew any kind of snake information might be valuable. He certainly did not want to encounter another one of those timber rattlers. The poisonous varmint's Latin name is even worst - "*Crotalus* (rattle) *horridus* (dreadful)." Joe planned to stick to his previous plan - leave the rattlesnakes alone and hope they would leave him alone. He could just see himself, alone on The Trail, trying to suck out the venom from the calf of his leg. He was not a contortionist and he doubted Houdini could even pull that one off. He just hoped those snakes would be asleep up under some rock.

And Joe found quickly that "a pound" of weight not needed was certainly a pound that needed to be subtracted. At the very start Joe tried to eliminate some of this extra baggage but even with the first adjustments he still started his long trip with a pack of over fifty pounds. Carrying fifty pounds a short distance on nice level ground is bother enough. Try maintaining such a load on treacherous mountain trails, around narrow rims of the sides of mountains and over ledges and rocks. The human body has a natural balance all by itself. Load it up at the top of your back with a fifty pound pack and you begin to look like a tottering robot that has not been programmed correctly. In other words, it's very difficult to keep your balance.

Joe compared his first night at the comfortable dry lodge with the second night which found him sloshing through the primitive remains of a great mountain range forest. A better term would be "rain forest." Joe had never seen so much rain. If it was going to be like this very much a fellow could get real discouraged about this hiking thing! No wonder about twenty-five percent of the hikers never made it past Neels Gap. They were probably dying with pneumonia - or worse.

Joe saw Thursday, March 25, 1999, come with just a sprinkling of rain and he was thankful for the coolness that came along with it. Joe camped at Woody Gap near Suches, Ga. Now, Woody Gap is an isolated place. The school there is even designated as an "isolated school." But its isolation serves a great purpose for its people. They pull together and are very close-knit. The last time I saw the figures for student population it stood at 112.

Now, about this time, Joe was feeling pretty "isolated" himself and he looked longingly for better times on the Appalachian Trail. But he knew it would be tough. And it was.

Joe camped at Woody Gap that night and wrote his last covered distance in his journal - 12.1 miles. So far he hadn't seen the first eastern milk snake, pileated woodpecker or pink lady slipper. But he really hadn't been looking for them.

Credits: Info of Joe Ward; Info of John David Harrell; Amicalola Falls info; Woody Gap info; personal notes; other sources.

Part 8
In The Mountains Of Georgia

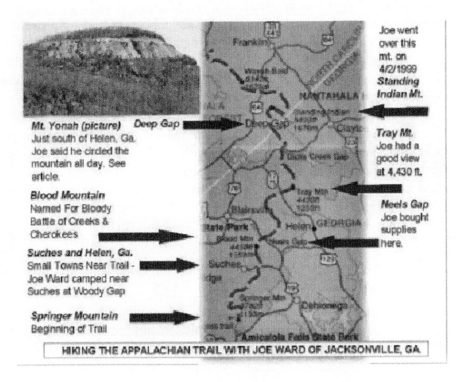

Mt. Yonah (picture) *Deep Gap*
Just south of Helen, Ga.
Joe said he circled the
mountain all day. See
article.

Blood Mountain
Named For Bloody
Battle of Creeks &
Cherokees

Suches and Helen, Ga.
Small Towns Near Trail -
Joe Ward camped near
Suches at Woody Gap

Springer Mountain
Beginning of Trail

Joe went
over this
mt. on
4/2/1999
*Standing
Indian Mt.*

Tray Mt.
Joe had a
good view
at 4,430 ft.

Neels Gap
Joe bought
supplies
here.

HIKING THE APPALACHIAN TRAIL WITH JOE WARD OF JACKSONVILLE, GA

Joe Ward of Jacksonville, Ga., hiked the entire Appalachian Trail - 2,160 miles, more or less. This map shows his starting point at the Southern terminus, Springer Mountain. As Joe hiked The Trail he passed interesting and challenging places. This map includes some of those places - on the first leg of Joe's trip - from Georgia to North Carolina.

Joe Ward was breaking camp at Woody Gap, Ga., and resumed his hike along the Appalachian Trail. But the sprinkling rain and the coolness of the day at Woody Gap was nothing compared to what Joe would find on Blood Mountain. The last time he was there it was just foggy and he couldn't see much. This time it was worse:

"Friday, 3/26/99 - Snow and sleet most of day. Hard snow on Blood Mountain."

Now, according to the information I have, Blood Mountain is 4,458 feet up in the air. That is nearly a mile straight up! It is amazing to me that Joe had the presence of mind to write anything in his trail journal. I think my binoculars would have been turned southward - hoping to find a small slice of passage that would take me to a land of no snow and warmer weather. But Joe was making a real try on this challenge; his eyes were turned northward and soon he would be clear of Blood Mountain and its cold slippery dangers.

From Blood Mountain Joe hiked toward Neels Gap. This was the nice place Joe and John Harrell had camped thirteen years before on their Georgia section hike of the Appalachian Trail. Joe was glad to see this place again because they had things you find in the civilized world - hot water, sleeping quarters, laundry, food, supplies, conversation, etc. It was the kind of place you hated to leave - knowing the next place you would find yourself would be out on the Appalachian Trail again.

Joe's journal tells us:

"Camped at Neels Gap to buy supplies and rain suit next day. Sent cotton clothes home. No good, too much weight."

Joe told me about the only thing he had on him that was any good was his Mastercard. It is amazing how plastic currency reaches into the hindmost parts of this country. But I am glad Joe felt secure with this substitutionary piece of financial wampum. In his situation the next place I would be showing my Mastercard would be the bus station - for a ticket indicating a location in south Georgia. But Joe was determined to give The Trail his best shot.

Now, Saturday is usually a day off for many of us - but not Joe. When you are on the Appalachian Trail you have to make the most of your time and make all the time you can and cover all the miles possible. You can't sleep much. If you don't discipline yourself and do these things you will, upon returning home, look like Rip Van Winkle and feel worse.

So, Saturday was just another day on the mountains for Joe:

"Saturday, 3/27/99 - Woke with snow everywhere. Real pretty. Stayed at Neels Gap until 1:00 PM. Got rain suit and replaced cotton clothes with capilene and wool socks. Camped just before Testatee

Gap. (5 mi.) Put up tent on slope and kept slipping to bottom of tent."

Now, the above entry needs some comment and expansion. To begin with I, probably like many of you, had no idea what "capilene" is. It is a product of clothing designed for people walking the Appalachian Trail - or other trails. You have to be thinking "light" to understand the below advertisement of the company trying to sell this product. You can see from the beginning that they are assuming that one wants to get as "light" as possible - even if it means forgoing certain personal garments:

"So ... you don't do underwear? These boxers might make a convert out of you. You'll get a silky-smooth layer between you and your Stand Ups -- without a hint of constriction. Made of Capilene Silkweight, the fastest wicking and drying of our base-layer fabrics, they are fun yet functional, with a relaxed, easy fit, --- etc."

I use that detailed description of Appalachian clothing, or lack of it, to point out the great importance placed on the shedding of any weight unnecessary to the conquest of The Trail. While this may seem like picking at straws to the common layman it is of critical importance to a hiker on the Appalachian Trail. That is why Joe Ward sent the cotton stuff back to Jacksonville, Ga., and resuited with Capilene.

Joe at this point is realizing the small details which go into making the big picture materialize into success. Joe pointed out to me quickly that there was a vast difference in toting a pack of 50 pounds versus one of 45.

And, Joe learned quickly to pitch his tent on level ground. The slanted version was sending his body on a slide to the lower end of the tent. He would remember the lesson and remedy the problem the next time. Those hillside mud-sliding Californians might repeat their mistakes but not Joe Ward. The next time the tent would be level and sliding around in his tent would not be the problem with getting a good night's rest. It would be something else.

Credits: Info of Joe Ward; Info of John David Harrell; Patagonia Clothing info; Wayne Busch photo credit for image of Mt. Yonah; personal notes; other sources.

Part 9
In Georgia With Kentucky Fried Chicken And Headed For North Carolina

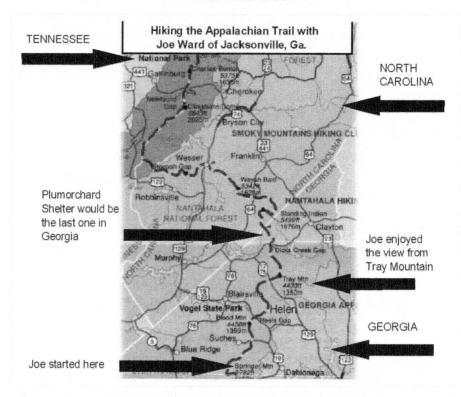

Joe Ward of Jacksonville, Ga., had made but a dent in hiking the Appalachian Trail. But, despite rain and snow, he was now making it out of Georgia and into North Carolina. He was also meeting friends on The Trail. Their advice and information would help him immensely as he continued to tackle his goal of hiking the Appalachian Trail. And he was supported by friends from his home in Jacksonville, Ga. He needed all the help he could get.

As Joe Ward slid to the bottom of his tent for the last time he realized it was Sunday. The concoction he bogged in was not chocolate icing or fudge - it was plain old mountain mud mixed with snow. What a mess! But today would find him going around (and around) Mt. Yonah, near Helen and Cleveland, Ga.:

"Sunday, 3/28/1999 - Made it to -- 3 miles from Unicoi Gap today. Camped near Rocky Knob shelter. Circled Mt. Yonah all day. Looked like it had me on a string. (12 mi.)"

Mt. Yonah has had a lot of people on strings in its long history. The Cherokee revered the mountain as a holy place. They held many ceremonies on its summit. Legend has it that a young Cherokee princess and a young warrior who were seriously in love jumped from the top of the mountain to their deaths rather than be separated. Now, that is true love, albeit short-lived. But their terminal encounter with the mountain does not stop droves of aspiring mountain climbers from trying to climb its sides.

By the way, if you go up there to climb you might have to give way to the Army Rangers who train on the heights of Mt. Yonah.

After circling Mt. Yonah all day Sunday Joe was glad to find some closure on that exercise. But the rain had not left entirely:

"Monday, 3/29/1999 - Woke up to sprinkling rain. Headed to Helen for supplies as soon as rain breaks. Twelve noon, caught a ride into Helen. Got package, made phone calls, washed clothes, and ate ice cream. Caught a ride back to trail in about 5 minutes. Made about 3.5 miles today. Had left my tent at Unicoi Gap before going into town."

John David Harrell, Joe's trail coordinator back at Jacksonville, Ga., was seeing to it that Joe received his mail packages. This was critical to the success of conquering The Trail.

Returning to his tent at Unicoi Gap Joe found himself with food and drink. Hikers were good about leaving groceries behind for their trail buddies. Joe enjoyed that Kentucky Fried Chicken. It was much better than any he had eaten in the flatlands!

With his fried chicken nourishment Joe was ready to tackle the path ahead. It would carry him over Tray Mountain:

"Tuesday, 3/30/1999 - Went over Tray Mt. today. Had a good view at 4,430 feet. I can still see Mt. Yonah. They say you can see Stone

Mountain (100 mi. off) on a clear day. There is a road to the base of Tray Mountain. Camped at Sassafras Gap with several other people. We had a fire. One of the others had thru-hiked before. I learned some from him. (10.4 miles)."

Joe had now covered some 60 of the 75 miles of the Georgia section of The Trail. He was lucky to come into contact so soon with a "thru hiker." A thru hiker is one who does the whole Trail. Many hike sections of The Trail but a thru-hiker goes all the way - the entire AT - some 2,160 miles, more or less.

Now, just what the thru-hiker told Joe I don't know. He could have told him that bears like Snickers so leave the chocolate candies at home. He probably told him that, unlike grizzlies, black bears can climb trees! Also in the free information could have been a mention of the rats mixed in there with the mice - those critters who besiege you at the shelters. I am afraid I would not sleep much with mice running across my face; and imagining one of those big rats nibbling at my toes. But whatever he told Joe I am sure Joe valued it. On the Appalachian Trail you can use all the information you can get your hands on.

I even saw a deodorant commercial tied to black bears. It gave three salient points: (1) Don't use perfumes (as bears are attracted to those significant smells); (2) Try to keep clean and not sweat; (3) Use the company's Unscented Deodorant!

It suddenly dawned on me that the conquest of the Appalachian Trail involves much planning, much maneuvering, the wise use of much information, and keeping a vigilant lookout for all potential troubles. "Be Prepared" is an understatement if ever there was one! And I suspect you had better be in pretty good physical shape - not to mention your mental status.

But regardless of all the above, the rain kept coming:

"Wednesday, 3/31/1999 - Woke to rain again. Fifth wet day so far out of eight. Rained all day. Made it to Plumorchard Shelter about 5:30 PM. It was packed but I squeezed in. First shelter I've slept in so far. Made 10-11 miles today. Hope to stay here a little while in the morning and dry out some."

Plumorchard was the last shelter in Georgia. Evidently Joe had not, at this point, been mauled by black bears, bitten by rats, or gotten lost in the torrential deluges of rain which beset him often. The rain might dampen his body and his spirit - but not enough to deter him from his attack upon his goal of hiking the Appalachian Trail. He would soon be in North Carolina.

The young man from Jacksonville, Ga., squeezed the water from his socks and smiled as the mice scurried back to their holes in the shelter. The daylight was here; they did most of their work at night.

Joe grinned again as he thought how good that ice cream was at Helen, Ga. - and also, he salivated at the thoughts of that Kentucky Fried Chicken. Such treats were few and far between.

Credits: Info of Joe Ward; Info of John David Harrell; Appalachian Trail info; personal notes; other sources.

Part 10
You Might See Anything Out Here

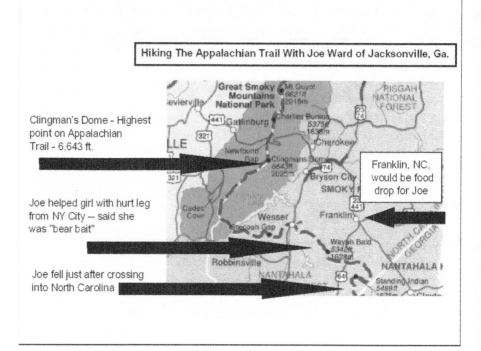

Hiking The Appalachian Trail With Joe Ward of Jacksonville, Ga.

Clingman's Dome - Highest point on Appalachian Trail - 6,643 ft.

Franklin, NC, would be food drop for Joe

Joe helped girl with hurt leg from NY City -- said she was "bear bait"

Joe fell just after crossing into North Carolina

Joe Ward of Jacksonville, Ga., hiked the Appalachian Trail. Many people hike sections of The Trail but relatively few hike the whole 2,160 miles from Georgia to Maine. Joe had his ups and downs on The Trail but he kept going. It is difficult to describe a person who hikes The Trail - they come in all sexes, ages and physical conditions.

Joe Ward had encountered wild turkeys near Jacksonville, Ga. He was glad to see they were active in the woods along the Appalachian Trail. A little wildlife scenery would certainly help break any monotony. As I read this entry of Joe's I thought about Fred Barrs here in Douglas imitating a turkey. Fred is a true sportsman and can tell a fine story or two about his adventures in the outdoors. Joe had come across a turkey caller on The Trail:

"Thursday - 4/1/1999 - No rain and warmer this morning. Left

about 10 AM. Everything still wet. Passed turkey hunter on trail. Followed him awhile as he called. Heard my first turkey gobble in woods. 1 PM : Reached Georgia/North Carolina line. One down."

Joe had hiked the Georgia part of The Trail so he said, "One down." The second state, North Carolina, was now the state to cross and Joe looked forward to the challenge. On the NC-TN border he would encounter the highest peak on The Trail, Clingman's Dome, 6,643 feet, in his conquest of this state. He knew he had a challenge in front of him. Talk about thin air!

The Appalachian Trail is no picnic path. Folks get hurt out there and unless you follow country singer George Jones's advice -- "these old bones they move slow but they're sure of their footsteps" -- you are liable to incur some pain. Joe Ward was not that old but he knew what it was to make a misstep.

"Fell this morning. Lucky I landed in soft spot. Got careless and lost balance. Camped just before Water Oak Gap about 2.5 miles before Deep Gap, N.C., where Johnny and I started 16 years ago. (9 miles today)."

As we said before, it is easier to tilt over when you are loaded down with a pack on the upper part of your body. Walking in hazardous areas would be difficult enough without the pack but the extra load at the top could easily be the little extra that tips you over. Especially if rocks are rolling beneath your boots.

Along about this time Joe was having nostalgic memories about the Georgia hike he and John Harrell had made sixteen years before - in 1983. They had covered the same portion of The Trail that Joe had now covered. Going on past this point would be new ground for Joe. He thought about how he would like to have John with him but the fire truck accident had deprived John of this opportunity. But John was serving an important role - he was coordinating Joe's hike from home base - Jacksonville, Georgia. John was essential to the success of the hike.

"Friday - 4/2/1999 - Pretty day so far. Everything is about dried out in pack now. Came through Deep Gap, N.C., this morning. Where Johnny and I started our trip."

But Joe knew there would be aggravations along the way:

"Insects are starting to be a problem. Left ankle is a little stiff. Everything else is fine. Went over Standing Indian Mountain (5,498 Ft.). There was six inches of snow on it last week. Stayed in shelter at Carter Gap. (11.5 Miles)."

Can you just imagine what it would be like out there - day after day after day? No fast food places, no city lights, no humming of vehicle tires on paved roads, no chatter of the crowd at the post office, the work place, or the church. No nothing. Silence except for the sounds of nature. And sometimes just silence. Just you and The Trail before you. Endless steps toward a goal that did have an end but it was hard to believe it.

But Joe was already thinking of that break that would allow him a bit of civilization again. It would come in the form of Franklin, N.C.:

"Saturday - 4/3/1999 - Only 16 miles to food drop in Franklin, N.C. Can't get it until Monday so I'll have two easy days to get there. Will go over 100 miles today (total miles since beginning hike of The Trail)."

Now, about the time Joe thought the silence and isolation would set in upon him there was always a surprise. Looking down The Trail he saw a damsel in distress. Now, he thought, what in the world is that girl doing out here in the middle of nowhere?

"Helped a girl get her pack down off Albert Mountain today. She was having problems with her leg. (Bear Bait from N.Y. City). Camped at Rock Gap shelter. (12 mi. today)"

There are brave and reckless souls out there on The Trail. I would just like to know what reasons this lone girl had for taking such a diversion from the usual routines of life back in New York. Was she tired of living in her boring surroundings or was she working on a thesis that required an actual stroll through the wilderness she now found herself in?

In any case, I think I would have brought along a friend. But like Joe, many find the solitude a source of strength and a place of reflection. The Trail seems to attract both sexes, all ages, and persons of various disabilities. One blind man hiked The Trail with a seeing eye dog!

Joe could see very well but right now he didn't know if that was an advantage or not. He was seeing some things that made him wonder. He was just trying hard not to bait any bears.

Credits: Info of Joe Ward; Info of John David Harrell; Appalachian Trail info; personal notes; other sources.

Part 11
Smoky Joe Didn't Want To Bait Smoky The Bear With Chocolate

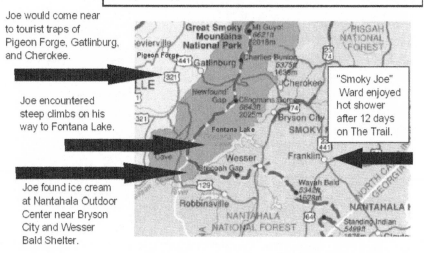

Hiking The Appalachian Trail With Joe Ward of Jacksonville, Ga.

Joe would come near to tourist traps of Pigeon Forge, Gatlinburg, and Cherokee.

Joe encountered steep climbs on his way to Fontana Lake.

Joe found ice cream at Nantahala Outdoor Center near Bryson City and Wesser Bald Shelter.

"Smoky Joe" Ward enjoyed hot shower after 12 days on The Trail.

Joe Ward of Jacksonville, Ga., was hiking the Appalachian Trail. By now he had picked up a trail name - Smoky Joe. The going continued to be rough but he kept hiking toward his destination - Mt. Katahdin in Maine. He had now hiked over 128 miles but had many more to go before his 2,160 mile trip ended. Joe had hardships along The Trail but he still managed to find ice cream occasionally.

Joe Ward took his time as he trudged toward his next goal on The Trail - Franklin, NC. He also wanted to nurse that slightly sore left ankle as much as possible. He certainly did not want to take any more falls. Next time he might not be as lucky. At Franklin he would hopefully receive a package from his home at Jacksonville, Ga. His mother, Helen Ward, and friend and coordinator, John Harrell, were trying their dead-level best to mail him the necessaries to keep him going. But sometimes communication failed and Joe just had to make the adjustments and keep traveling:

"Sunday, 4/4/1999 - Caught a ride into Franklin, NC, this morning. Staying in motel ($32) until morning to get food. Several others from trail did the same. Hope to get an early start in the morning. (4 mi. today. Total 110 mi.) Go Smoky Joe."

That same day Joe wrote his mother and John Harrell a card telling them not to worry about the supply connection not working:

"Sunday, 4/4/1999 - (CARD) Dear Momma and Johnny, Made it to Franklin, NC, today about noon. I'm staying at a motel tonight. First shower in 12 days. Have made 110 miles now. Talked to Murray (Joe's brother) today and he said you had not gotten my card yet. Don't worry, you should get it in time and if not I can buy something. In addition to food changes I made on last card, add 10 or 12 of hot chocolate (Sweet) and 12 packs of instant oatmeal. I can't get used to warm milk."

Joe knew he had to watch that sweet chocolate. Smoky the Bear would be after the chocolate of Smoky Joe Ward. Bears love chocolate. But a man had to eat and drink and the hot chocolate would taste good. But the last thing Joe wanted to do was bait a bear!

Joe continued his instructions to his home base at Jacksonville, Ga. His mother and John Harrell would be anxiously awaiting his note to them:

"Send to Mountain Momma's, 1981 Waterville Rd., Newport, TN, 38821. ETA (expected time of arrival) 4/17/1999. Hope everyone is fine. Love, Joe. PS - Send books #2 and #3."

A note from John Harrell to Joe explained what had happened with the mails:

"Card had been sent to Broxton, Ga., before it came here. That is why it was late; also I had sent book #2 to Franklin, NC."

Despite these minor difficulties, Joe rose fresh to go the next morning. The rest and relaxation at Franklin had made a new man of him. He was now ready to again confront the challenge of the Appalachian Trail.

"Monday, 4/5/1999 - Day 13 - Left Franklin, NC, about 10:00 AM. Camped at Licklog Gap. (12.5 miles). Need to try to keep this pace and

be at Fontana Dam Friday night."

The discipline of The Trail somehow found itself manifested in a hiker's mental odometer/speedometer. A thru-hiker knew he had to make a decent amount of miles per day to be successful. If he fell short one day he knew he had to make it up. Somehow the calculations were there and a hiker was aware of that built-in distance/speed recorder.

But despite his new fresh start from Franklin and an optimism that rivaled the bright sunshine around him, Joe soon found that Nature was trying to dampen his spirit and body again with the onset of moisture falling from the skies:

"Tuesday, 4/6/1999 - Day 14 - Rain again. Camped at Wesser Bald shelter (new) approximately 10 miles. Got everything dry."

Now, about this time Joe was thinking how nice it would be if the original plan for the Appalachian Trail had been funded and implemented. That plan called for nice shelters with hot and cold running water, laundry facilities, and other amenities. Unfortunately, there were but a few of those scattered along the length of The Trail. Most were rather crude structures that barely got you by, if that. It was good to see this new shelter at Wesser Bald. At least it was new and provided shelter and water. It allowed Joe to dry out his stuff.

Joe lifted his long lanky frame and looked north and south from his vantage point at 4,115 feet elevation. At Wesser Bald Shelter he was now 2,038.7 miles from his goal of Mt. Katahdin in Maine. But he had clocked 128.4 miles from his beginning point at Springer Mountain in Georgia. He was making progress! Go Smoky Joe!

Joe was glad the left ankle was doing better because he knew he had some rough trail before him. He sure would like to find some ice cream:

"Wednesday, 4/7/1999 - Day 15 - Hiked to Wesser, NC, and Nantahala Outdoor Center. Bought a few things I needed and ate ice cream. Approximately 30 miles to Fontana. Very tough section of trail - long and steep climbs. Camped at Sassafras Gap Shelter. 13 miles."

This was the second Sassafras Gap encountered by Joe. He had already passed one down The Trail in Georgia.

Joe was tempted toward second thoughts. Those cool waters of the Nantahala River looked so inviting. Maybe he should switch to whitewater rafting. But he knew better - the challenge of The Trail lay before him.

Credits: Info of Joe Ward; Info of John David Harrell; Appalachian Trail info; personal notes; other sources.

Part 12
Placing Hiker And Food Relative To Bears Seems To Be Reversed

Joe Ward of Jacksonville, Ga., reaches the Smoky Mountains on his way along the Appalachian Trail. Joe had his doubts, at first, about the reported beauties of the Smokies but as he progressed he found the views to be breathtaking. That big pack on his back had to be a heavy companion. "Smoky Joe" is moving along The Trail quite well now despite many inconveniences.

Cousin Thomas Wayne Anderson, Lt. Col. (Ret.), US Army, wrote me a note supporting what Joe Ward said about the steep climbs in the mountains along the Appalachian Trail. He has been following the recent Appalachian Trail articles on the Old Jacksonville, Ga., website and relates the following:

"The Appalachian Trail hike has been enjoyable. I have some familiarity with the North Georgia sector from my days in U.S. Army Ranger training. During the winter of 1967-1968, I attended and

completed Ranger School. The mountain phase north of Dahlonega was especially challenging. Mountain climbing was not my forte; however, I enjoyed rappelling down. We did a whole lot of walking around in "them thar hills." And, it was cold, especially the river crossings. The way to travel on foot is to follow the ridge lines once you get up to them. The problem is that the ridges do not always follow the direction you are heading."

I certainly appreciate Cousin Thomas Wayne writing in his comments. Now I am assured someone out there is sharing the Joe Ward experience of hiking the Appalachian Trail. When we were children I would visit Cousin Thomas Wayne at his home in the Workmore community north of Jacksonville, Ga. I never pictured him hanging off one of those Appalachian mountains. You can just never tell where that ridge will lead!

Speaking of ridges, Joe Ward was still looking for one because at the moment he was going almost straight up:

"Thursday, 4/8/1999 - Day 16 - Hiked 11.5 miles to Cody Gap and camped. Tough climb. Going into Fontana tomorrow."

Joe had heard of the beauty of the Smoky Mountain National Park and he certainly wanted to get there. The angles on these hills were getting to be quite tiring. The gobble of a turkey interrupted his thoughts:

"Friday, 4/9/1999 - Day 17 - Just before dark yesterday PM I heard a turkey gobble. I called back and he gobbled every time I called. Made it to Fontana about 4:00 PM. Going into town in the morning. Caught up with hiker I had met earlier on the trail - Louis Fritz "Elf" from Nebraska A very interesting man. Retired school teacher in his mid fifties. He has run seventy marathons but said the Appalachian Trail is the toughest thing he has ever started. 9.3 miles today."

Finally, Joe is nearing the Smoky Mountains and is anxiously awaiting the experience:

"Saturday, 4/10/1999 - Day 18 - Got up before daylight this morning. I stayed in shelter at Fontana Dam. Had 2nd shower in free public showers. Heard coyotes and turkeys at daylight. Went into town this morning for food and started into the Smoky Mountains. It's supposed to be one of the prettiest sections. It should take about six

days and I'll have close to 250 mil. One tenth of the way."

The break also gave Joe a chance to write home to Jacksonville, Ga., and tell the folks back there of his progress:

"Saturday, 4/10/1999 (CARD) Momma and Johnny, It's just breaking daylight as I write this. I'm looking at the lake formed by Fontana Dam. I'm hearing coyotes howl and turkeys gobble while I'm drinking my coffee. Got here yesterday afternoon and stayed in shelter here. There are public showers so I had my 2nd one in 17 days. Everything is good. Still a lot of rain. Next food drop - Erwin, TN 37650. ETA 4/25/1999. Love, Joe. PS - Start Smoky Mountains today. 166 mi. down."

You can tell by his entry in his trail journal that Smoky Joe Ward is in this endeavor to complete it. After all the rain, missed food, delays, aggravations, lack of bathing opportunities, and general deprivation of all that comes with the routines of living, Joe still says, "Everything is good." Something tells me Smoky Joe is ahead of the game - mentally and physically. Go Smoky Joe!

"Saturday, 4/10/1999 - Left Fontana about 1:00 PM, crossed the dam and started the Smokies. It's supposed to be really something but so far it looks the same. Only made 5.2 miles today to first shelter. This was the plan because in the Smokies you have to stay in or by a shelter with your food behind a wire cage to keep the bears out."

Now, this plan I would not care for. As I understand it, when you arrive at the shelter with your food in tow and the shelter is full you have to sleep on the outside of the shelter and put your food in a wire cage inside the shelter! Somehow I get the feeling they have things reversed here. As far as I am concerned they could put the food outside and let the bears go for it and I would get in the wire cage on the inside!

I am beginning to see - more and more - why the trek along the Appalachian Trail is described as somewhat of a challenge.

Credits: Info of Joe Ward; Info of John David Harrell; Info of Thomas Wayne Anderson; Appalachian Trail info; personal notes; other sources.

Part 13
Shelter Was Full – Smoky Joe Outside With The Bears

Joe Ward found it mighty cold up there around Clingman's Dome, highest point on the Appalachian Trail. That funny looking stuff on the ground and hanging in the trees was called hoar frost. See article for more on Smoky Joe Ward of Jacksonville, Ga., hoar frost, hungry bears and other interesting info about the Appalachian Trail.

The bears were probably watching Smoky Joe Ward sweat it out as he pondered his chances of getting a place inside the next shelter. Regulations in the Smoky Mountains part of the Appalachian Trail required you to stay in a shelter. And if the shelters were full the regulations required something even worse!

The following entry gives us a hint that Smoky Joe Ward was somewhat anxious about this situation:

"Sunday, 4/11/1999 - Day 19 - Early start this morning. Planned to do 16 miles but only made 9.7. Would like to do more because I got to this shelter at 3:30 PM. Next shelter was 6.3 miles but I didn't feel up to it. Have to stay in or at a shelter while in the Smokies. Shelters have strong wire front to keep out bears. Most sleep twelve people and are filling up. Only three thru hikers can stay in a shelter if there are nine section hikers. If it fills up thru hikers have to pitch tent outside but leave food in shelter. So far I've gotten a space in the shelters. So far the Smokies haven't been any prettier than the rest and the shelters are a lot fuller. I don't particularly like this."

What I wouldn't particularly like would be sleeping out there on the outside of the shelter with the bears trying to crawl over me to get to the food which was stored on the inside of the shelter! I would be afraid they would get frustrated and take out their hunger pangs on me!

I know Joe was relieved when he saw deer instead of bear the next day:

"Monday, 4/12/1999 - Day 20 - Cold this morning. (Mid 30's) Windy and cool all day but good hiking. Saw two deer at shelter this morning. They would let you get within a few feet. One doe and one buck that had just shed his antlers. Got some good pictures. 13.5 miles today."

Our picture of Joe today shows him surrounded by hoar frost near Clingman's Dome. He told me it was a beautiful sight. The authorities on hoar frost tell us:

"Hoar frost occurs when water vapor touches a very cold surface and freezes on it instantly. This can happen to the leaves and branches of plants, and will cover them with ice crystals that look like spiky fingers."

Now Joe is about to climb to the highest point on the Appalachian Trail - Clingman's Dome:

"Tuesday, 4/13/1999 - Day 21 - Third week out and I feel good. Another cold night and morning. (Mid 30's) Frost in trees and freezing in pot when I washed them. Going over Clingman's Dome today. Will hit 200 mile mark today. I've changed my mind about the Smokies. They are getting very pretty and stay at a high elevation. Around 5000 feet plus. So it is staying cool. Ice in places all day long."

The history of Clingman's Dome is very interesting. The following information is from the Smoky Mountains National Park Service:

"Rising 6,643 feet above the Great Smoky Mountains, Clingman's Dome is the highest point along the Appalachian Trail and provides a 360° view of the surrounding mountains. From it's 54 foot observation tower the average viewing distance is about 22 miles, but on a clear pollution free day, views can amplify as far as 100 miles into 7 states. The mountain was named after the Civil War General/US Senator, Thomas Lanier Clingman, a prospector who obtained much wealth from the timber and minerals of this region. Clingman originally measured Mount Mitchell as the highest peak, which of course it is at an elevation of 6,684 feet, but Dr. Elisha Mitchell also made this claim and after much debate and a decade later Mitchell went back to remeasure the mountain and fell to his death at the base of what is now known as Mitchell Falls. Clingman agreed that because of this tragedy Mount Mitchell should be named after Dr. Mitchell; therefore, the highest peak in the Great Smoky Mountain National Park was named after Mr. Clingman and is located on the state line ridge of North Carolina and Tennessee, the observation tower sitting equally in both states."

Unfortunately, Smoky Joe Ward could not make reservations at a shelter. It was like a race which included him, the other hikers, and the bears! This time Joe was to lose that race and had to stay outside with the bears. I think his statement, "It was a strange feeling" must rank right up there with the top ones for being nominated as Understatement of the Year.

"Shelter was full this evening so I had to put up a tent outside of shelter. It was a strange feeling. Had to put my food bag in shelter and have the people inside lock the door behind me to keep the bears out. 13.8 miles today."

The next morning Joe checked himself over good to see if he still had all his appendages. Fortunately the bears had left him alone and he was physically, if not emotionally, intact. A little sleepy perhaps - owing to the fact that he slept with both eyes open! That certainly makes sense. You can't see those bears coming with your eyes closed. Little wonder that he records an energy level drop in his next entry:

"Wednesday, 4/14/1999 - Day 22 - Left early this morning. Didn't feel very energetic today. Got a space in shelter for the night. (12.6 miles today)."

But Joe was heading for better times. Mountain Moma's was just ahead and a cheeseburger feast awaited Smoky Joe. And maybe even a little ice cream.

Credits: Info of Joe Ward; Info of John David Harrell; Info of Smoky Mountains National Park Service; Appalachian Trail info; personal notes; other sources.

Part 14
Erwin, Tennessee – Where They Hanged An Elephant

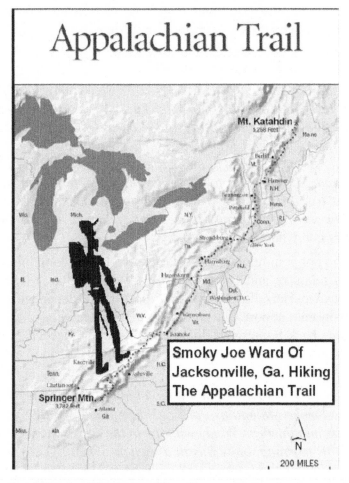

Appalachian Trail

Smoky Joe Ward Of Jacksonville, Ga. Hiking The Appalachian Trail

Smoky Joe Ward of Jacksonville, Ga., now is about a tenth of the way to completion of The Appalachian Trail. He has experienced the great beauty of the Smoky Mountains National Park. He has also experienced the hardships of trail living and hiking. He cannot doubt himself or the goal he has set. Mountain Moma's gives him food and rest.

Burnout! This was something Smoky Joe Ward wrestled with as did other hikers on The Appalachian Trail. I read somewhere that only about 10 percent of the thru hikers who start The Trail finish it. Joe knew in his heart that his mindset had to be stable to accept the environment he was now facing. After all, this was no halfhearted traipse up Pig Mountain at Jacksonville, Ga. The conquest of The Appalachian Trail was a monumental task, completed only by those enduring souls who pushed to the limits and who abandoned the thoughts of their air-conditioned homes and the other amenities of civilization. Joe did not want to burn out:

"Thursday, 4/15/1999 - Day 23 - Late start today (11:00 AM). Hard rain last night and this morning. Lucky I was in a shelter. Only did 7.1 miles to next shelter. That is good because I need a rest. Going into Davenport Gap and Mountain Moma's tomorrow for food drop, shower and real food. I had planned to make it in tonight but I've been doing 12 and 13 mile days for a while and it's catching up with me. Don't want to burn out. It's a long way to Maine. Food is real low because I'm staying out a day longer than planned. I hear Mountain Moma's has good food."

Joe's line of communication to Jacksonville, Ga., kept him in close touch with relatives and friends. Especially his mother, Helen Ward, and John David Harrell, his hike coordinator. He depended on these people for moral support and physical support. Knowing they were at their stations back home gave Joe the assurance he needed. They also provided listening ears. This was also important. Here Joe writes them a card:

"Card - 4/15/1999 - Momma and Johnny, This should be my last night in the Smoky Mountains Park. It's been really pretty. Some cold nights in the mid thirties. Windy with ice in the trees. Rained hard last night and this morning, but I was in a shelter. When I get to Mountain Moma's Friday for food drop I will have been 236 miles. A little over one tenth of the way. Food drops are going good. Next one after Erwin, TN, will be Damascus, VA 24236. ETA 5/5/99. I'm spreading them out now but plan to pick up some food along the way at close stores. Love, Joe. PS - Go back to whole jar of peanuts.

The mental odometer in Joe's head was keeping track of miles. His mind was also tracking the days on The Trail. It was also measuring and calibrating his journey - the progress he had made and the remaining part. He was now over a tenth of the way. Nine tenths to go! Go Smoky Joe!

In talking with Joe about Erwin, TN, he did not realize it had a history of elephant hanging. Once a circus came to town and an elephant stepped on her cruel trainer. Rumors spread and soon the poor creature was targeted as a stampeding leviathan - wiping out all humanity in its path. Not true but little good it did Mary, the unfortunate elephant. They hanged her from a derrick (crane). Probably something the town is not real proud of today (but tourists pay for the story and pictures!). If you are interested in more of that story see Old Jacksonville Article No. 214 (I can send it to you).

Notice in the P.S. that Joe asked that his whole jar of peanuts be reinstated. Hikers often cut back on quantities of various items in order to lighten their load. One hiker said toting a back pack from Georgia to Maine was like going the distance with a bag of cement on your back! Hikers come up with all kinds of ways to lighten their load. Some even shave off the ends of their toothbrushes to reduce weight!

I have heard of people who were deprived of food for some time and upon having the opportunity to eat, overdid it. I almost believe Joe Ward fit this category after he described his assault on Mountain Moma's food menu:

"Friday, 4/16/1999 - Day 24 - Made it to Davenport Gap about 1:00 PM and walked about one mile down road to Mountain Moma's. Ate all afternoon. Big cheeseburger, fries, apple pie, ice cream, three oatmeal pies, milk, big apple, cheese, and two cokes. Got food drop, washed clothes and had shower. Put up tent by pretty stream and slept well."

It is difficult to tell just how important Mountain Moma's is to the thru hiker. Scores of hikers have soaked in the amenities of that establishment and the best way to describe the famed stop is to allow another hiker to put it into his own words. This account comes from Kurt and JoAnne and it seems they, like Joe, experienced the indescribable balm of the Appalachian oasis known as Mountain Moma's:

"I am very glad we stopped here at Mountain Moma's Kuntry Store. Part of the fun of long-distance hiking is experiencing the local

culture along the way, and Mountain Moma's is quite the piece of Americana. From the 3 junk cars parked next to the satellite dish, to the neon cigarette sign that says "Jesus is Lord", to the Dolly Parton shrine, this is about as local as you get. You cannot sit down outside without a dog or cat jumping into your lap or sleeping at your feet. The shower water smells horrible (like sulfur), but with some soap it got 5 days worth of grime off me. JoAnne says they gave her the same water to drink with dinner (which explains why she suddenly changed her mind and bought a soda)."

Now, mind you, Smoky Joe Ward might have had about the same thing to say about Mountain Moma's but he was not in the mood for lengthy narrative. He was too busy ordering up a big breakfast; he had a busy day ahead and needed more nourishment. Go Smoky Joe!

Erwin, TN
Where They
Hanged An
Elephant

Credits: Info of Joe Ward; Info of John David Harrell; Info of Smoky Mountains National Park Service; Notes from Kurt and JoAnne; Appalachian Trail info; personal notes; other sources.

Part 15
Smoky Joe Met Up With A "Trail Angel" And Two Old Soldiers

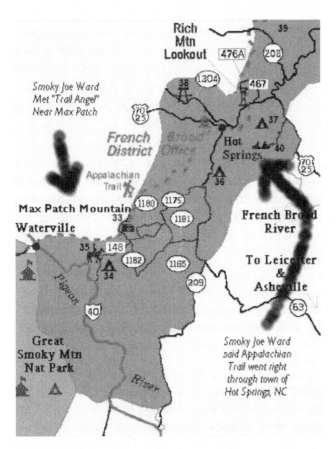

Smoky Joe Ward was making progress along the Appalachian Trail. In today's article he made his way to one of the beautiful mountain "balds." On the way there he met a "Trail Angel." He came across memorials placed to the memories and deeds of men who came there years before for different reasons. [Photo credit: Trail Map - Pisgah National Forest Service]

Mountain Moma's place had been an oasis on the Appalachian Trail. Joe enjoyed the company of the other hikers and he feasted on the food the place afforded. Following the huge consumption the day before Joe was now ordering breakfast:

"Saturday, 4/16/1999 - Day 25 - Big breakfast this morning. Pancakes, eggs, bacon and coffee. Gonna catch ride back up to trail and head north. Need to start making more miles each day. I'd like to start doing 15 miles a day soon. Another sunny cold day with a little snow this afternoon. (12.6 miles today.)"

We continue to see the pressure Joe put on himself to make more miles per day. Somewhere in his resolve to hike The Trail Joe placed emphasis on keeping a good pace. Maybe it was the rhythm of this momentum that carried him relentlessly toward his goal. Maybe it was the realization that he was still "making his miles" as planned. It could have been the fact that if he got too far behind schedule and arrived at Mount Kahtadin, Maine, too late there was the possibility that it would be shut down - closed - because of the severe and forbidding winter conditions! Whatever it was, it appeared to be working. Smoky Joe was serious about reaching his goal. He did not want to return to Jacksonville, Ga., without the dirt of Mt. Kahtadin, Maine, on his boots.

Folks talk about the beauty of the "balds" of the mountains. These are great grassy clearings. Joe Ward was on his way to one of these famous features. When he got there he would have a panoramic view of the world around him. On the way there he was also to meet a "trail angel."

"Sunday - 4/18/1999 - Day 26 - Slept good last night. Cold with a little ice rain falling on the tent. Had a good experience this morning. Came to a place called Max Patch Mountain. A big grassy mountain once used to graze sheep and cows. Just before getting to the top I came to a couple of loop trails and got on the wrong trail. The trail I took led to a public road. While I was trying to figure out where I was a truck pulled up and a boy got out and asked me if I was thru hiking. He turned out to be what people on the trail call "Trail Angels." Someone who has hiked the AT before and likes to bring food to hikers. He gave me a ham and cheese sandwich, coke, pop tart, Little Debbie Cake and a banana. I ate it all. He also told me how to get back on the trail. I wouldn't have seen him if I hadn't got lost. Not sure about miles today. I think I did about 15 miles. I'll have to see tomorrow when I know where

I am. (15.4)"

As long as Joe could make these 15 mile days he felt like he was making steady progress. Most of the time he would have to leave The Trail to get into town. Not today though. The Trail was going right through the next town:

"Monday - 4/19/1999 - Day 27 - 15.3 miles today. Into Hot Springs, NC, today. Trail went right through town. Got a new sleeping bag - longer and lighter. Also got a light that goes on my head. Very useful. Spending a lot more money than I had planned, but I'm getting some good equipment Ate pancakes and bought some candy bars and pop tarts. I'm eating a lot when I go into town. Two 15+ mile days in a row. I need to try to keep this pace if I can hold up. Four more 15 mile days will get me to Erwin, TN, Friday afternoon for Saturday food drop at post office. Total miles 280.3. "

But the 15-mile days were taking a toll on Smoky Joe. There was a fine line between doing too little and doing too much. But he shifted gears to adjust his hiking to match his energy:

"Tuesday - 4/20/1999 - Day 28 - Last two days of 15+ miles have worn me out. Don't need to push too hard. Today the hills seemed higher and my pack felt heavier. 13.3 miles today. May not make Erwin by Saturday morning. If not I'll spend Sunday night and get food Monday morning. Hate to lose days but I need to rest."

Joe Ward saw some interesting things on his hike. He even came across memorials to men who had been along that same way. Some for the same purpose he had and others for reasons far different:

"Wednesday - 4/21/1999 - Day 29 - Today at approximate 300 mile mark I came by a small memorial to a man (83 years old) from Connecticut who died in 1987. He hiked the whole trail in 1968. His family spread his ashes on the mountain. Trail followed several old roads today. I always try to imagine what kind of traffic was on those roads 100 to 150 years ago and how people lived in those mountains, etc. At one point I passed two graves of Civil War soldiers. I'm only hiking these mountains, but they were marching all over the country. Camping and fighting terrible battles when they got to where they were going. Makes my trip a little easier. Felt better today. (15.1 miles today, 308.7 total.)"

The Trail had made Joe weary. As he shut his eyes that night for a deep sleep he thought about those old soldiers again. He could almost imagine hearing "Taps" as he drifted off in satisfying slumber.

Credits: Info of Joe Ward; Info of John David Harrell; Map of Pisgah National Forest Service; Appalachian Trail info; personal notes; other sources.

Part 16
Smoky Joe Believes Friends And God's Help Will Get Him To Maine

Joe Ward relaxes with two of his trail friends near Erwin, TN. After you have been on The Trail you acquire a "trail name." "Snail" is on the left, "Sunshine" is playing with the cat and "Smoky Joe" Ward is on the right. They are staying at a place called "Uncle Johnny's." Years ago an elephant was hanged at Erwin, TN, but Joe Ward of Jacksonville, Ga., didn't have elephants on his mind when he went through Erwin, TN.

Joe Ward missed Jacksonville, Ga. His days and nights on the Appalachian Trail were nice but he thought of home and the ones there. But he knew he must maintain a regimen and make his miles. If he didn't he would never make it to Maine.

"Thursday - 4/22/1999 - Day 30 - Hit the trail at daylight. Needed a big day so I can make gap at Erwin (TN) tomorrow. Did 17.6 miles. Most yet. Probably too much but now I only have 14 miles to do tomorrow. Plan to stay at Nolichucky Expeditions and campground. Showers and shuttle service to Erwin for food drop. (326.3 miles)"

Joe had arrived at a famous (or infamous) place. Years ago a circus came to Erwin, TN, and a tragic thing happened. An abused elephant named Mary stepped on her cruel trainer and sentence was passed on the unfortunate pachyderm. Mary was hanged from a crane and died right there in front of a huge crowd. It was her last show on earth. But driving by the neat houses of the old pottery town one would never guess its regretted past.

Friday - 4/23/1999 - Friday - Day 31 - One month on the trail today. Made it to Erwin, TN, or the gap at Nolichucky River four miles from Erwin. Everyone pitched in $5.00 and had hot dogs and hamburgers. I had 3 hot dogs, a hamburger, 2 cokes, and a bunch of chips. Campground had showers and washing machine. Will catch a ride into town in the morning for food at P.O. and maybe a haircut and try to get back on the trail by early afternoon. Raining some tonight. Hope it clears. (12.7 miles today. Total 339)"

On The Trail Joe had moments of reflection which included pleasant thoughts of home and the ones who were helping him make his dream come true. John David Harrell, his hike coordinator, was one of the important persons in Joe's world. John could not come on the hike because of a fireman's accident which broke both legs. Joe writes to his friend:

"Friday - 4/23/1999 - Day 31 - Johnny, I'm writing this after talking with you on the phone. I'm in the tent after eating hotdogs and hamburgers - no ice cream. I always feel like I forgot to tell you something when I call because I'm usually trying to think of a lot of different things I have to do. I just want to let you know how much it means to me having you help me. I just wish you could be here too. It seems like a long time ago that you let me out in the rain at Springer Mountain and drove off. That was sort of a lonesome day climbing that mountain in the rain and wondering what I was getting myself into. I still have some tough days, but I believe I like it better every day. With your, momma's and God's help I believe I'll make it to Maine. Thanks for being a friend. Smoky Joe. Next food drop Bland, VA 24315, ETA 5/12/1999."

But Joe had to be flexible. Sometimes his food was not at the post office. Plan B had to always be there to do battle with his disappointment. Today was another of those days when things didn't work out:

"Saturday - 4/24/1999 - Day 32 - Food didn't make it to Erwin. Must be lost somewhere. Bought some food and left town about 3:00 PM. Post Office is to forward package to Elk Park, NC. Wasn't sure how long it would take to get there but it should be only three days from here. May have it sent home. Late start today. Only 4.2 miles. Total 343.3"

Food not arriving was only one of Joe's problems - a physical one. But he was having to contend with psychological effects - seeing fellow hikers trying to find ways to beat The Trail. He was beginning to see more and more hikers fall out and go home. He hoped he would never be among that number.

"Sunday - 4/25/1999 - Day 33 - 14.2 miles today. Lots of climbing. Wanted to do 15 miles but found a good campsite and that's close enough. Should get to Elk Park, NC, early enough Tuesday afternoon to get to post office for food. I've been seeing several hikers lately who have started "slack packing." Walking the trail but getting someone in a car to take their pack to the next road. Others are also "blue blazing." Taking different and shorter trails. Some I started with have quit. Total today 357.5 - Average 10.83."

We continue to see the mental gymnastics of Joe as he reassures himself and challenges himself with the numbers he has put up. He has to keep going. The numbers made in good time matter. He must not lose sight of his progress expressed numerically. That is the proof of the pudding.

"Monday - 4/26/1999 - Day 34 - Early start, 7:00 AM. A light drizzle as I packed up tent. Wanted to have a good day so I could get into Elk Park Tuesday night or Wednesday morning. Light rain all day and some tough climbing. By mid afternoon I was wet and cold and decided to stop at a shelter short of the one I had planned to make. It was so rainy that I missed the shelter and went another four or five miles to the next shelter. (16.4 miles). During the night my food bag fell and hit another hiker in the head - (Big Daddy). You have to hang your food up to keep the rats out. Total miles 373.9."

I hope Big Daddy had a great sense of humor. I know Joe saw little humor in the advance of the rat army. Eating your food after the rats had nibbled over it would take some doing. I would have been reviewing the Greyhound bus schedule for points south. But Joe was not giving up. He had committed himself to hiking the Appalachian Trail.

Credits: Info of Joe Ward; Info of John David Harrell; Appalachian Trail info; personal notes; other sources.

Part 17
Daniel Boone Blazed These Trails In Virginia

Smoky Joe Ward of Jacksonville, Ga., pauses on another mountain as he crosses it. Joe is now getting into the beautiful land of old Virginia. Years ago Daniel Boone blazed trails through this country. Abingdon, VA, and Damascus, VA, are beautiful places to visit. But they look a little different from the window of an air-conditioned tour bus as compared to the view seen by a hiker of the Appalachian Trail.

Joe Ward stopped by the house the other day and we chatted quite a bit about his hike of the Appalachian Trail. I could tell Joe didn't care much for the shelters. Besides being plagued by the rats and mice, there wasn't much room for modesty in using the restroom facilities. Many times they were open on one side and both sexes had to do the best they could under the circumstances. Joe said when a group was there it was a bit uncomfortable when a person headed for the john but as time wore on he got more accustomed to the reality of being in the woods and not having the same routines as afforded by civilization beyond The Trail.

I could tell though that he was never completely comfortable with those arrangements. I am quite sure those in the shelter tried to avoid eye contact with those in the privies. Especially if those in the shelter were trying to dine.

But such was life on The Trail. You just had to try to make the best of a bad situation. Anyone contemplating hiking the Appalachian Trail should realize right off that conditions are not in any way comparable to the comforts of life "back home." That is probably why there is such a great dropout rate on The Trail. Trying to get back to those comforts of civilized living!

But back to Smoky Joe on The Trail. We left him in a shelter when his food bag fell and hit "Big Daddy" on the head! This was in a shelter somewhere between Erwin, TN, and Elk Park, NC. Evidently things went OK and he departed to continue hiking.

"Tuesday, 4/27/1999 - Day 35 - Decided on short day today. 9.9 miles to make shelter just before road to Elk Park. I will go into town early in the morning and hope to get back on the trail by lunch. Very pretty hike today. Total miles 383.8."

At this point Joe is enjoying the hike as the terrain is getting a bit easier to travel over. Joe said some of the toughest climbs were in Georgia. As he approached Virginia the going was smoother and he was enjoying the great views. He was glad Georgia was behind him.

"Wednesday, 4/28/1999 - Day 36 - Last night after I had already eaten a big supper some other hikers came back from Elk Park with pizza. I had two big slices of pizza. This morning I caught a ride into town. My package still hadn't arrived so I had it sent home. I bought enough food to get to Damascus (not exactly what I needed because it was a small store) and got back on the trail a little after 10:00 AM. Had a big breakfast in town before leaving. Only did 12 miles. I was tired for some reason. Don't want to push too hard."

I know that Joe was now in some pretty country. Damascus, his next main objective, is near Abingdon, VA. Anyone going through there on a tour bus has experienced the beauty of the place. You also probably took in one of the performances at the old Barter Theatre there. But Joe's perspective, for sure, was not from the tinted window of an air-conditioned tour bus.

"Thursday, 4/29/1999 - Day 37 - Started raining sometime during the night. Only a light drizzle by morning. Tent is leaking somewhere plus condensation. Got to do something about this. Light rain and cool all day. Stopped at old barn (log cabin) this afternoon to get out of rain and eat snack. It was real cozy and dry. Short day again today (9.8 miles). Wanted to stop at a shelter to get out of rain and dry things out. Stayed at Laurel Fork Shelter. Pretty place on a high ridge above a creek. I really enjoy my days better when I'm not so worried about my mile average. I think they will pick up when I hit some easier sections. Don't want to overdo it. Total miles - 405.6."

Now, about the time I thought Joe was rid of those pesky little mice, here they come again. I don't think I could have slept at all under the conditions described by Joe:

"Friday, 4/30/1999 - Day 38 - 15.4 miles today, total 421. Staying in a shelter again. Had a bad time with mice last night running over my face. Got up during the night and put my tent up in the shelter. Tonight I'm doing the same. No stakes or poles, just tie the front up with a rope."

Joe was now approaching "the friendliest town on the Appalachian Trail." Here around Damascus and Abingdon, VA, Daniel Boone blazed trails and put the old towns on the map. Here the trails of Boone and others make the place a mecca for hikers. You can hike or ride a bicycle. Joe probably wished he had a bicycle about the time he came upon this point in his travels.

"Saturday, 5/1/1999 - Day 39 - 18.4 miles today, total 439.4, average 11.26. Fairly easy walking today. Not a lot of bad climbing. About 15 miles into Damascus, VA, tomorrow. A church runs a hostel there. For just a few dollars you can get a bunk and shower. I need to wash clothes too. There is a good outfitter there and I may get a tent."

Sore feet, dirty clothes, leaky tents, aching muscles and mice tracks across your face. And a bunch more things that would make most of us yearn for home. But Smoky Joe Ward of Jacksonville, Ga., just grinned and kept walking. He had mountains to climb.

Credits: Info of Joe Ward; Info of John David Harrell; "Damascus, VA - Friendliest Town on the Appalachian Trail"; First Baptist Church; Appalachian Trail info; personal notes; other sources.

Part 18
Damascus, Virginia - The Friendliest Town In The Appalachians

Smoky Joe Ward and
The Wild Ponies Of
Grayson Highlands
State Park -
Appalachian Trail

Smoky Joe Ward of Jacksonville, Ga., enjoyed the wild ponies of Grayson Highlands. He said they really didn't seem that wild. About this time Joe probably would have liked one tame enough to ride. He had done a lot of walking and had more than that to go. He was about one-fourth distance-wise along the Appalachian Trail. The Trail was taking its toll on Joe but he was hanging in there.

Joe Ward found himself in "the friendliest town in the Appalachians" - Damascus, Virginia. He hoped the store personnel there would also be friendly and helpful because he needed a tent. He hoped they would also help him economize if possible. You have to watch your money hiking the Appalachian Trail because things can get expensive. They sort of have you over a barrel because you can't always run down the road and do comparison shopping.

"Sunday, 5/2/1999 - Day 40 - Into Damascus about 4:00 PM. Got a bunk in a Methodist Church hostel for two dollars. Had a shower, washed clothes, and ate pizza and ice cream. Looked at tents. May get one in the morning. 14.9 miles today, 454.3 total, average 11.35."

But Joe found the tent a little more costly than his night's stay at the Methodist hostel.

"Monday, 5/3/1999 - Day 41 - 9.4 miles today, 463.7 total, average 11.3. Bought a new tent this morning ($220). Hope I like it and it keeps me dry. Got mail drop and left town about 12:30 PM. Only made it to first shelter. Wanted to set tent up and seam seal it but didn't. Maybe tomorrow. If tent stays dry I'll like it."

A note home from Joe let the folks know how he was faring and his location:

"Card 5/3/1999 - Momma and Johnny, About to leave Damascus, VA. Everything going well. Next drop Catawba, VA 24070. ETA 5/21. Love, Joe."

Joe was trying to make as many miles as possible per day but he also had to be aware of taking care of business. This included getting his tent in good shape. After all it was his home away from home.

"Tuesday, 5/4/1999 - Day 42 - 13 miles today, 476.7 total, average 11.35. Would have gone farther today but wasn't sure about water and camp sites. Also wanted to set tent up early and apply some seam sealer. Got my rain fly on upside down tonight so I could seal the bottom side."

The expression "wild horses couldn't keep me away" seemed appropriate for Joe's next stop. He was about to witness the wild ponies of Grayson Highlands State Park.

"Wednesday, 5/5/1999 - Day 43 - 16.6 miles today, 493.3 total, average 11.47. Very pretty section today. Took lots of pictures. Part of trail went through Grayson Highlands State Park where they have wild ponies. I saw several and got some good pictures. They were really pretty tame. They have an auction every September to keep the numbers down. Also went over Mt. Rogers (5,729 ft.), the highest point in Virginia on the Appalachian Trail (I think!). I made it to a shelter tonight because it looked like rain but the shelter was full. I didn't have

enough seam sealer to do the whole tent yesterday but I think it will be o.k. I'll see! I'll hit 500 miles tomorrow."

It is interesting to see how Joe reacted to and handled adverse weather conditions.

"Thursday, 5/6/1999 - Day 44 - 14.1 miles today, 507.4 total, average 11.53. Hard wind and rain early this morning. Tent stayed dry. Always hard to start a day in the rain. Can't cook breakfast. Have to pack everything wet. That's all part of it and I've been pretty lucky so far not getting caught out in the rain."

It is also interesting to see how he adapted to various types of people on the trail. Sometimes these individuals were loud - the last thing you wanted to hear after a hard day's hike.

"Friday, 5/7/1999 - Day 45 - 14.8 miles today, 522.2 total, average 11.6. Today didn't go as planned, as usual, but worked out good. I was only going to do 10.5 miles today and stay at partnership shelter. It's at Mt. Rogers National Recreation Center and has a shower and pizza place in town that delivers. I got there about 1:30 PM and went to the visitors center. I ate four candy bars and drank two Pepsis I went back to the shelter and unpacked for the night. Late in the afternoon a lot of young hikers started coming in. From being around them before, I knew they would be loud all night About 3:30 PM, without my shower, I got back on the trail. About 30 minutes after leaving I ran into a bad thunder storm. It also hailed some. After about four miles of this it let up a little and I was able to get my tent up. It's still raining now but I'm warm and dry. Tomorrow about 7.5 miles from here the trail goes right by a restaurant and small store so I'll eat good and resupply some."

Joe's next entry made me think of the Blands of Jacksonville, Ga. It is said their roots are up there in Virginia.

"Saturday, 5/8/1999 - Day 46 - 10.1 miles today, 532.3 total, average 11.57. Rained very hard last night and my new tent stayed dry. I'm real happy about that. Made it into town today and bought a little extra food to make it to Bland, VA. Also went to the Dairy Queen and had a big cheeseburger and an Oreo Blizzard. Also ate some M&M's before leaving town. Got back on trail but only did about three miles."

Now, everything was smelling good to Smoky Joe Ward today. But tomorrow was going to be a stinker.

Credits: Info of Joe Ward; Info of John David Harrell; "Damascus, VA - Friendliest Town on the Appalachian Trail"; United Methodist Church; Appalachian Trail info; personal notes; other sources.

Part 19
Some Of The Bland Family Found At Virginia

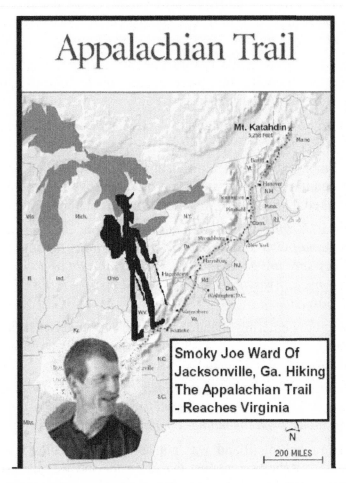

Appalachian Trail

Mt. Katahdin
5,258 Feet
Maine

Berlin
Vt.

Hanover
N.H.

Bennington
Pittsfield   Mass.

Wis.   Mich.   N.Y.   Conn.   R.I.

Stroudsburg
New York

Pa.

Harrisburg   N.J.

Ill.   Ind.   Ohio   Hagerstown

Md.   Del.
Washington, D.C.

W.V.   Waynesboro
Va.

Ky.   Roanoke

N.C.

Smoky Joe Ward Of
Jacksonville, Ga. Hiking
The Appalachian Trail
- Reaches Virginia

Tenn.

S.C.

Miss.

N
200 MILES

Smoky Joe Ward of Jacksonville, Ga. (inset) keeps moving along the Appalachian Trail. He is now in Virginia. Joe runs up on a dead skunk and the sight and smell were breathtaking. It didn't take him long to enjoy enough of that scene. But he had some better moments in this section of the country. His visit to Bland, VA, brought to mind the Blands of Jacksonville, Ga.

Whew! Joe Ward sniffed the air and quickly realized he had come upon an odoriferous environment. Things were smelling bad! He could possibly imagine someone or something killing a rabbit or a squirrel or even a bear. But a skunk?!

"Sunday, 5/9/1999 - Day 47 - 14.1 miles today, 546.4 total, average 11.63. Hit one-fourth of way today. Good hiking and good weather. Good camping spot except it smells a little because something killed a skunk close by."

Wondering briefly what reward goes with killing a skunk Joe hit The Trail again. Leaving this place behind would be a pleasure. The farther he went the fresher the air got.

"Monday, 5/10/1999 - Day 48 - 16.1 miles today, 562.5 total, average 11.72."

Now Smoky Joe found himself at the next scheduled post office stop. He liked to make these stops and pick up news from home and he especially liked it when there was food from his mother's kitchen!

"Card 5/11/1999 - Dear Momma and Johnny, Just got into town and got my mail. I'm sitting outside the post office eating Momma's muffins. They sure are good and still fresh. Got a lot to do in town so I won't write much. Everything is fine. Next drop - Tyro, VA 22976, ETA 6/2/1999. Love, Joe."

Joe was now entering Bland, Virginia. The Blands of Jacksonville, Ga., probably drifted down from that area into North Carolina and then to Georgia. We found a little on the history of the county:

"The county was named after Richard Bland, a leader of Colonial Virginia whose arguments laid the intellectual foundation for freedom and independence from the mother country."

Another rebelling Bland was not as fortunate. Giles Bland took part in Bacon's Rebellion against the governor and was hanged for it. He was really tricked into surrendering upon promise of a pardon. But the governor was afraid to let him live. Some time ago some of us from Douglas, Ga., got a chance to visit the old home of Giles Bland.

So now Joe Ward of Jacksonville, Ga., was entering this domain of the old Bland family. It was a place of many interesting happenings, both large and small. As a matter of fact, at one time in Bland County you could get a twenty-five cents bounty for every crow you killed and fifty cents for every chicken hawk.

But crows and chicken hawks were the last things on Joe's mind. Joe was tending to business and that included getting food. A man walking The Trail needs good nourishment.

"Tuesday, 5/11/1999 - Day 49 - 12.3 miles today, 574.8 total, average 11.73. Into Bland, VA, for food drop. Very easy to catch a ride into and out of town (2.5 miles each way). Town trips are always hectic for me. Too much to do and having to run all over town. It's nice to have food waiting for me though. I've started buying a little extra food because I'm eating more cheese, bread, cookies, etc. My pack is really heavy when I leave town. I only went about a mile out of town today and camped. I think I may be on private property but it was not posted. Found out later that I was on U.S. Forest Service land."

But Joe was doing good. He was enjoying the ridges of Virginia although up there you better have a supply of water. And water weighs a lot, especially when you are carrying it around in a back pack.

"Wednesday, 5/12/1999 - Day 50 - 14.8 miles today, 589.6 total, average 11.79. Getting my daily average up close to 12 where it needs to be. Should hit 600 miles tomorrow. So far Virginia hasn't been too rough. Do a lot of walking on ridge tops and not quite as much climbing as in Ga., N.C. and Tenn. I still get a good workout every day. One bad thing about ridges is that there isn't as much water and I have to carry more - usually about a half gallon. It's also harder to find places to camp with water. Last night I was camped in a grassy, open area and after I had gone to sleep I heard something walking around the tent. It turned out to be several deer, but it scared me for a while."

The next entry of Joe's confirms that the area around Bland, VA, truly has elements in common with Jacksonville, Ga. I wonder what the hounds were chasing. One old-timer from Bland, VA, told a story years ago and said that some dogs up there were treeing a possum but when they pulled the thing out of the tree it was a mink! They got seventy-five dollars for him.

"Thursday, 5/13/1999 - Day 51 - 18.9 miles today, 608.5 total, average 11.93. Felt like I was at home in Jacksonville last night. I could hear hounds barking down in the valley. Saw my first groundhog

or woodchuck several days ago. I didn't know they were in Virginia. Got into another thunder and hail storm this afternoon. Made a long day to get to next shelter."

The Old Dominion State - Virginia - had Joe feeling pretty good about his long hike. Tomorrow he was going into Pearisburg and with some luck would get to stay in a motel overnight. He felt he was due some comfort. The Trail takes its toll and Joe was ready for a moment of relaxation. At least maybe they wouldn't have any dead skunks. Whew!

Credits: Info of Joe Ward; Info of John David Harrell; Info on City and County of Bland, VA; Appalachian Trail info; personal notes; other sources.

Part 20
Smoky Joe's Mother Helped A Lot Of Us

Smoky Joe Ward had now arrived in Pearisburg, Virginia. This old photograph of the town reflects how it looked in Civil War days. Evidently it had made some changes by the time Joe arrived because he stayed at a motel there. The Appalachian Trail goes right through the town. Joe tells us that the flowers and trees were blooming and that things were looking up. He had now completed over 600 miles of The Trail. [Photo credit: City of Pearisburg, Virginia]

Smoky Joe Ward was still remembering that dead skunk he got a whiff of back on The Trail. But he would get to see many animals on his trek from south to north on the Appalachian Trail. There was a variety of animals and plants. According to Bill Bryson, a famous trail walker, some wildlife expert had said there were about 300,000 mammals on a typical area of ten square miles in these mountains. He even broke that down: 220,000 mice and other small rodents, 63,500 squirrels and chipmunks, 470 deer, 30 foxes, and 5 black bears. And an unidentified number of live and dead skunks! I would say that was a pretty good statistician to come up with that count. I'm glad he was counting and not me.

Joe was looking for some plants, too. His father, Bro. Wade Ward, was an admirer of nature and I think Joe was like him in this respect.

"Friday, 5/14/2005 - Day 52 - 8.3 miles today, 616.8 total, average 11.86. Into Pearisburg, VA, today. Trail runs right through town."

It seems Joe liked it when The Trail ran right through a town. This way he didn't have to make a side trip off The Trail to get into town for supplies. And a nice comfortable motel was usually right there in the town.

"Staying in motel tonight (second one). Need to buy a few things, wash clothes, etc. Looking forward to a hot shower or two and some good food - probably pizza. Had three candy bars and a coke as soon as I checked in."

Joe was delighted that nature was about to show its colors big-time. It seemed to help his attitude about the long hike.

"Everything is starting to bloom and turn green now (Dogwoods and Honeysuckles). Rhododendrons haven't started yet but should be pretty. Nice change from everything looking like winter. It's really nice to see the seasons change. Hopefully I'll see some fall colors at the end of my trip."

When Joe got a chance he would also fax messages to his home in Jacksonville, Ga., so his folks would know his status. It was good to stay in touch - especially when you were in such a remote area. Joe smiled when he thought some folks might think Jacksonville, Ga., was in a remote area. But it was home to him and his current surroundings were not.

"Fax from Pearisburg, VA - 5/14/1999 - Hey, I'm in Pearisburg, Va. The trail goes right through town so I'm staying in a motel tonight. (Just my second one). It's 616 miles to here so I'm making progress. Everything is going fine. I got your package in Bland, Va. The muffins were still real good. I ate some as soon as I opened the box and later I got a quart of milk and ate some more. I gave a few to some hikers."

If you are hiking the Appalachian Trail you encounter a special kind of camaraderie out there. Folks tend to share their food. You never know when that can be a most fortunate arrangement. It is tough at best. Cooperation makes it a little more bearable.

"I got caught in a bad thunder and hail storm yesterday and got real wet and cold, so I walked 19 miles to make it to a shelter for the night. I need to buy a few things in town, wash clothes, etc. It'll be good just to relax. I'll probably leave about noon tomorrow. Call me back at 540-921-0129. PS - Let me know how Uncle Dink is doing and how I can write him."

Even on The Trail Joe was concerned about his kin and friends. He also got a note from Johnny Harrell (his hike coordinator) back in Jacksonville, Ga., concerning another event of sadness in the community. Johnny had told of going to Mr. Edgar Burch's funeral. He also informed Joe that Mrs. Ward (Joe's mother) had gone to her sister's in Albany, Ga.

You just can never tell about the weather on the Appalachian Trail. Joe was cautious about getting rid of warm clothes as is reflected in this note home:

"Letter to Mrs. Ward (mother) from Pearisburg, Va., Saturday, 5/15/1999 - Hey, another book and 617 miles behind me. Thinking about sending some of my warmer clothes home, but every time I do it gets cool again. Better wait awhile. Hope you are doing good and enjoying the Braves. PS - Some cards, etc., are in this book. Love, Joe"

Mrs. Helen Ward truly enjoyed watching the Atlanta Braves. Mrs. Helen Ward was a special lady. When I was about fifteen years old Mrs. Ward was the Personnel Manager for Royden Wear, Inc., probably the largest employer in McRae, Ga., at the time. The large factory made and shipped garments. She gave me my first "paycheck" job. Of course, I had made a little money picking cotton, gathering scrap iron, selling catfish, and working in my father's store, etc., but I had never been hired at a place that had you on the payroll and made all those sophisticated-looking deductions. I worked some on the day shift and part of the time on the night shift. Tom Steverson and I made the daily/nightly trek to McRae to work in the shipping department of that clothing concern. Mr. Henry Selph was our foreman and we thought the world of him. And Mrs. Wade Ward (Helen), Joe's mother, was the person who gave me this great opportunity. I learned what responsibility was all about in the world of manufacturing and commerce. I also learned how to work with other people. It was a great experience.

Now, Joe's mother was helping him succeed - succeed in walking the Appalachian Trail. Of course, she was also enjoying the Atlanta Braves, too.

Credits: Info of Joe Ward; Info of John David Harrell; Appalachian Trail info; "A Walk In The Woods" by Bill Bryson; personal notes; other sources.

Part 21
Selling His Idle Jeep And
Monitoring Precious Water

Smoky Joe Ward was leaving the comfort of Pearisburg, Virginia, and hitting The Trail again. Fatigue was creeping into the picture and he couldn't figure it out. Water also was not in abundance. He had to be careful - physically and mentally. Joe admired the flowers and trees but the Chestnut wood of this old rail fence was some of the last of its kind. The beautiful Chestnut tree had become extinct. [Photo credit: Picture of the Day Homepage]

Smoky Joe Ward had hunkered down in Pearisburg, Virginia, and was enjoying his stay. It is amazing to see that not only was he keeping up with the rigors of The Trail but he was also taking care of business back home. For some reason he was wanting to sell his Jeep. His Jeep was back at Jacksonville, Ga., and Joe probably thought that he might as well sell something he wouldn't be using for quite some time.

The following is a continuation of a note to his mother, Helen Ward, concerning the Jeep and other items:

"8:45 AM Saturday -- I'm at the post office in Pearisburg waiting for it to open at 9:00 AM so I thought I'd write some more. Didn't get a fax from you at motel last night so I'm thinking you may be gone for the weekend. Maybe I'll have one when I check out later this morning. Just wanted to hear from you.Johnny may have said something to you about selling my Jeep. If someone wants it I think I can call the bank in Douglas where I borrowed the money on it and they will let you sign the title over to whoever buys it. We'll see. Joe."

But Joe's hike coordinator, John David Harrell, was already ahead of the game. Johnny had kept the selling of the Jeep in the family:

"Johnny's note -- I had already sold the Jeep to my brother Marion for $3,000. The title would have to be sent from Atlanta to the bank and then to Mrs. Ward and she would sign it over to Marion."

As Joe pulled out of Pearisburg and onto The Trail he again felt the surge of the wild infuse his frame with a trickle of adrenaline. His eyes also adjusted again to the wilderness around him. He could see how the plant expert Bartram and others like him got excited at the flora of the new continent. The Indians must have looked at these botanists with amazement as the explorers showed their excitement over the newfound plants. Reminds me of the story of one scientist who visited the Broxton Rocks right here in Coffee County. It was said the rare plants there excited him so he was hyperventilating! It just takes different things to excite different people. As Joe crossed an old rail fence made of Chestnut wood it pained him to think of the sad fate of the Chestnut tree. It was now extinct. Gone forever from the American landscape. No more of these fences would be made.

But Joe had to balance the beauty of the flowers with his need for water. A person doesn't need to dehydrate on a mountain. I found that out one summer in Phoenix, Arizona, when one of our group went up the Camelback Mountain and ran out of water. He was in foul shape when he returned. I think that might have broken him from mountain climbing. But Smoky Joe was monitoring this water thing. He knew it was important.

"Saturday, 5/15/1999 - Day 53 - 8 miles today, 624.8 total, average

11.79. Out of town today a little before noon. Only went 8 miles so I could camp with water. Not a lot of water in this section because I'm staying up on ridges mostly."

Joe had a good day on Sunday and made 15 miles. Days like this helped his schedule because it pulled his average up and kept him on his projections. It was OK every now and then to linger in a town and eat a little too much ice cream but you had to pay for it later. You had to make up those miles.

"Sunday, 5/16/1999 - Day 54 - 15 miles today, 639.8 total, average 11.85."

But the mystery of fatigue always haunted Joe and he never could quite figure out the "tired cycles." He thought of his daddy, Rev. Wade Ward, striding over the terrain around Jacksonville, Ga. He never remembered his father saying anything about being tired. Maybe it was different up here in the higher altitudes.

"Monday, 5/17/1999 - Day 55 - 14.3 miles today, 654.1 total, average 11.89. Tired this afternoon - more than usual. Going to take it easy for a few days. Three days to Catawba for food drop. Still having to be careful everyday about water. Not many sources."

Worrying about water would be enough to make a hiker tired. Picture yourself walking ten or twelve miles with hopes of a drink of water at the end - only to find there was none.

The next day Joe cycled back to a better feeling. He really didn't know what to make of the changing ebb and flow of his stamina levels.

"Tuesday, 5/18/1999 - Day 56 - 12.3 miles today, 666.4 total, average 11.92. Eight weeks out today. Felt better today, more energy. Hard to figure it out. Some days are better than others. Saw some goats on the trail today. Must have gotten loose and gone wild. They were in a pretty remote and rocky place. Still think I should take it easy for the next few days."

But Joe was trying to make it to a small store just ahead on The Trail. When he got there he got some good news and he got some bad news. But it wasn't anything he couldn't handle. After all, he was now a mountain man and mountain men just keep going - tired or not.

Credits: Info of Joe Ward; Info of John David Harrell; Appalachian Trail info; "A Walk In The Woods" by Bill Bryson; personal notes; other sources.

Part 22
Tough Rocks, Friendly Wild Goats, An Angry Bad Bird And Some Deer

Smoky Joe Ward said the hiking was a little rough on Dragon's Tooth.

Smoky Joe Ward keeps finding challenges on the Appalachian Trail.   Climbing Dragon's Tooth was one of them.   The Jacksonville, Ga., native ran up with wild goats but they were friendly.   But he also ran up with an angry bad bird.   The bird wasn't so friendly.

After admiring a bunch of wild goats Smoky Joe Ward continued his journey. Luckily the goats didn't bother him as they did one hiker. The hiker reported one of the big animals almost pushed him off the side of a mountain. He said the goat looked to be three or four feet tall and probably weighed around 90 pounds. Only the walking stick of the hiker saved him when he jabbed the advancing goat with the end of it. It appears you can run up on about any type of adventure when hiking the Appalachian Trail.

But right now Smoky Joe was trying to make it to a little store on

The Trail. He had heard that the owners would let you camp there. That was good news. But the good news did not last long.

"Wednesday, 5/19/1999 - Day 57 - 16.4 miles today, 682.8 total, average 11.98. I was trying to do 16 miles to a small store but they no longer let you camp. Bought a few things, Snickers, Fig Newtons, and some drinks and got back on the trail to camp with Sky Dog, Snail, Bai-Dai and Poopa Jack. Went over a mountain today called the Dragon Tooth and it was some of the roughest, rockiest climbing I've done. I had to crawl over some of the rocks. Into Catawba today for food drop. There is supposed to be a good home cooking style restaurant in town (The Home Place). Sounds good to me."

Joe was ready for some good home cooking after Dragon's Tooth. What Joe had climbed over was an outcropping of quartzite. He was probably lucky to come out of that experience with no cuts or bruises. This is the way Dragon's Tooth is described in one of the trail references:

"The Dragon's Tooth is a unique geologic feature located atop Cove Mountain on the Craig/Roanoke County line. Dragon's Tooth consists of spires of Tuscarora quartzite which outcrop on the top of Cove Mountain. The tallest "tooth" projects roughly 35 feet above the surrounding rock. The trail to Dragon's Tooth ascends steep, rugged outcrops of quartzite which form the spine of Cove Mountain and North Mountain. The spine is known as Dragon's Back. A difficult hike, Dragon's Tooth summit offers magnificent views of nearby and distant peaks year-round."

Joe noticed the blooming of Spring on The Trail. He was also keeping in touch with his mother and John David Harrell, his hike coordinator.

"Card - Thursday, 5/20/1999 - Momma and Johnny, Into Catawba, Virginia, today. Weather is very nice. Rhododendrons are blooming on the trail. Very pretty. Hope everyone is doing well. Next food drop - Linden, VA 22642, ETA 6/14/1999. Total miles as of today 688.5"

Trail guides and books are important to a trail hiker. Joe communicates with home base concerning these references:

"Note to Mrs. Helen Ward, Thursday, 5/20/1999, Catawba, VA. Momma, I'll probably need some of this back in a couple of months.

I'm using a small trail book that covers the whole Appalachian Trail - The Appalachian Trail Data Book. I think you have a copy. You won't have to send me any more books. Might need to spread sleeping bag out. The stuff bag goes with it when I get it back. I've still got warm clothes so I hope I'll be warm enough. I found the watch."

John Harrell, his hike coordinator, also made a note:

"Joe had sent his sleeping bag and some small items including a watch he had found on the trail. I had ordered the Data Book. I hope it will help me keep track of Joe on the trail. Thing are looking real good if the weather will just cooperate."

It is interesting to note that some folks are friendly around the Appalachian Trail. When a hiker leaves it to go into one of the local towns for food or other reasons some driver usually picks him up and gives him a ride back to The Trail:

"Thursday, 5/20/1999 - Day 58 - 9.5 miles today, 692.3 total, average 11.94. Rhododendrons are blooming now and they are real pretty. I'll try to get a good picture. Left Catawba about 3:00 PM. Only a mile back to trail. I got about half way back and someone stopped and gave me a ride. Went about four miles to campsite."

Like we said, you can run across about anything on the Appalachian Trail. Now Smoky Joe comes into a confrontation with a bad angry bird. He didn't know quite what to make of it:

"Friday, 5/21/1999 - Day 59 - 12 miles today, 704.3 total, average 11.94. Short day today. Set up tent at 3:30 PM. I'll cross a highway tomorrow in about three miles where there are restaurants so I plan to be there for breakfast. Today on the trail a grouse flushed up right beside me and ran at me a couple of times before flying off like it was hurt. It must have been trying to get me away from its nest. I've seen quail do this but never had one try to attack me. Hit 700 miles today. Almost one third of the way. Last night was the first night without a sleeping bag and it was a little cool. Hope it warms up. I may need a blanket. I saw several deer today. I called one back around to me after it ran off. It was a young buck. It got pretty close to me but ran off before I could get a good picture. I took one but he had moved off some."

Well, Smoky Joe has now covered about one-third of the Appalachian Trail. He's a bit skinnier than when he started but he's doing OK. And, too, he has spotted some more food.

Credits: Info of Joe Ward; Info of John David Harrell; Appalachian Trail info; Perry McKay's account of "South to North"; Mike's Page photo of Dragon's Tooth; personal notes; other sources.

Part 23
Smoky Joe Staying Positive In Spite Of The Negatives

Smoky Joe Ward (inset) of Jacksonville, Ga., hiked the entire Appalachian Trail. Here is one of the scenes along The Trail but let's hope that is not Smoky Joe out there on the edge of that rock. It looks like that would be a long fall. But Smoky Joe had plenty of challenges without creating any new ones. The nights were still cold, even in May, and he had sent his sleeping bag home. [Photo credit: Mike's Page - The Appalachian Trail]

Smoky Joe Ward was aware of the challenges of the Appalachian Trail. Bill Bryson, a noted writer, had chronicled his own experiences with The Trail - "a lot of long, taxing miles, steep rocky mountains, hard shelter floors, hot days without showers, unsatisfying meals cooked on temperamental stoves." Joe smiled as he thought of the descriptive writing of one who had trudged over some of these same mountains and who had also tasted the negatives. But there were also positives.

"Saturday, 5/22/1999 - Day 60 - 3.5 miles today, 708.1 total, average 11.8. The trail crossed 420 (highway) today, near Daleville and Cloverdale, Va. I had planned to get a good meal and a few supplies and keep going, but I really felt like a good rest so I decided to get a motel room."

Joe's ability to see his journey as a whole, and in divided parts, resulted in a balanced itinerary. By breaking it up into reasonable hike and rest periods he was able to keep going at a fairly good pace and also relax some. This gave him a great edge and the variety in the schedule helped body and mind. He liked this work and reward system.

"Also today marked just about one third of my trip. Only had about 3.5 miles to motel from camp so I checked in about 9:00 AM. It's about 1:00 PM and I've washed clothes and eaten some candy and pizza. I've lost so much weight I need to eat all I can. I need to get a few supplies and then I'll watch TV and rest."

Joe not only watched his calories but he watched the weather. The weather can get you in minutes in the mountains. It can change quickly and have you in trouble before you know it.

"Sunday, 5/23/1999 - Day 61 - 11.2 miles today, 719.3 total, average 11.79. Easy day out of town. Left about 10:00 AM. Hiked to a shelter because there was supposed to be bad weather tonight. It's 7:30 PM now and the skies are clear. Thought I ate too much in town but my energy was good today so I must have needed it."

Although it was still cool to Joe, even in May, he could remember Bill Bryson's warning about summertime:

"There would be all the perils that come with warmer weather: Wild and lively lightning storms, surly rattlesnakes, fever-inducing ticks, bears with appetites, and, oh, one unpredictable, motiveless, possibly drifting murderer, since reports of the deaths of the two women killed in Shenandoah National Park were just making the news."

A chilling reminder of what could happen on The Trail. Not so comforting. And speaking of "chilling," Joe was finding the nights very chilly. He was not used to this sort of thing. Camping on the Ocmulgee River banks this time of the year would be warm aplenty.

"Monday, 5/24/1999 - Day 62 - 16.2 miles today, 735.5 total,

average 11.86. Long day today. Skipped a shelter that didn't have a water source and went on to a road with a creek running under a bridge and camped by the creek. Don't normally like to camp by roads but this one doesn't seem to have much traffic. Some kids were swimming and fishing."

But Joe was not deceived by the pleasant sight of youngsters swimming in the daylight hours and enjoying the warmth of the sunshine. At night things were vastly different. He had acted too quickly in sending his warm sleeping bag home.

"Tuesday, 5/25/1999 - Day 63 - 14 miles today, 749.5 total, average 11.9. Lots of climbing today. Back up over 4,000 feet. Has been cool every night since I sent my sleeping bag home. Tonight I'm staying in a shelter and if it gets too cold I'm going to cover up with my tent. Hard to believe it's cold the end of May."

Joe wanted to believe it was getting warmer but he knew in his heart it was cold. He was just trying to make the best of the situation at hand.

"Wednesday, 5/26/1999 - Day 64 - 12.4 miles today, 761.9 total, average 11.9. Stopped early today at a shelter (3:00 PM). Could have gone on but I won't be able to make Tyro by Saturday morning for my food drop, so I'll take it easy and get there Monday morning. Pretty shelter with a nice stream in front. It's 6:00 PM now and so far I'm by myself here. It's warmer tonight."

As Joe rested that night, wrapped in his tent, he could hear the sounds of nature around him. He knew it was getting warmer yet the chilling cold seemed intent on sticking around to make hikers uncomfortable at night.

He was alone tonight but tomorrow he would see another of his old trail buddies. They seemed to appear and disappear on a rather regular basis. But he was always glad to see them pop up here and there.

Credits: Info of Joe Ward; Info of John David Harrell; Appalachian Trail info; Bill Bryson's 'A Walk In The Woods'; personal notes; other sources.

Part 24
Smoky Joe Loved Ice Cream As Much As Stonewall Jackson Loved Lemons!

Smoky Joe Ward was crossing many beautiful streams with beautiful bridges along his way on the Appalachian Trail. He crossed the Little Wolf Creek (above) and now he is camping at the Tye River (inset shows suspension bridge there). The sound of the rushing water provided good background music for a good night's sleep. [Photo credit: Buck Nelson]

Smoky Joe Ward of Jacksonville, Ga., sometimes hit lonely venues along the Appalachian Trail and longed, from time to time, to see fellow human beings on The Trail. He was about to do that:

"Thursday, 5/27/1999 - Day 65 - 13.7 miles today, 775.6 total, average 11.93. Met back up with a boy (Groove) that I haven't seen since the Smoky Mountains. He had taken some time off to see his girl friend. He said another boy (Spectrum) was close behind. He had also

taken some time off. I'm sleeping warmer now but I'm wearing all my clothes and my rain suit and covering up with my tent when I'm in a shelter. I thought it was summer time. I may freeze in Maine."

The unpredictable weather situation kept Smoky Joe guessing. His attempts to stay relatively comfortable and adequate were also getting expensive. It was nice to see good weather:

"Friday, 5/28/1999 - Day 66 - 8.8 miles today, 784.4 total, average 11.88. Short day today. Nice weather. Shouldn't be too cool tonight. Staying in shelter again."

Joe's feelings of elation were beginning to show in his trail journal. Here was a young man who was about to conquer half of the Appalachian Trail with no signs of permanent damage to his lanky frame or mental carriage. He knew he was doing pretty good for a country boy used to the environment of the Ocmulgee River Valley. All that now seemed a good ways off. And it was.

"Saturday, 5/29/1999 - 15.8 miles today, 800.2 total, average 11.94. Eight hundred miles today. What else can I say? Into Tyro, Virginia, tomorrow for Monday morning food drop. 199 miles to Harpers Ferry, West Virginia, which is considered the traditional half-way mark although I won't actually be half-way until somewhere in Pennsylvania - Pine Grove Furnace State Park. Pine Grove General Store at 1,088 miles is home of the "Half Gallon Club" where you have to eat a half gallon of ice cream to mark the half point to belong to the club. I think I'll join up."

No better reward loomed on the horizon than the prospects of an abundance of ice cream. If you wanted to satisfy the palate of Smoky Joe just wave a little ice cream in his direction. He was already daydreaming about the various flavors of one of his favorite dishes. It was hard to beat plain vanilla.

"Sunday, 5/30/1999 - Day 68 - 11.7 miles today, 811.9 total, average 11.93. Down to Tye River and highway that runs into Tyro, Virginia, today. "Fanny Pack," a 1996 thru hiker was at the road with hamburgers, hotdogs, cookies, and cold drinks for all the hikers tht came through. He also drove me to town for ice cream. I saw "Spectrum", "Field and Stream", "Slugger", and "Single Matt"."

This brief respite of food and fellowship did a world of good for

Smoky Joe. Especially the ice cream. The State of Virginia had been good to him and he had enjoyed its beauty and hospitality. But he must push on beyond its borders. Harpers Ferry had to be up there ahead somewhere. Meanwhile, it was time to write home and connect with his mother and hike coordinator John David Harrell. Helen Ward and Johnny Harrell had helped him immensely with this challenge of hiking the Appalachian Trail.

"Sunday, 5/30/1999, Note to Mrs. Ward - Dear Momma, I'm camped on the Tye River at a road crossing that goes into Tyro, Va. I'll go into town in the morning for my food drop. The Post Office is in a small country store and even though tomorrow is a holiday I'm supposed to be able to get my package. Johnny said you were going to have to buy more food before long. Maybe you should just buy a few weeks supply at a time when you need it because I'm spreading them farther apart now and buying extra food along the way. I don't know how much more to tell you to buy. When you do buy more you can buy the same things that you've been sending. You may want to buy oatmeal in big boxes and put two cups in a bag and send four bags (Quick Cook). It may be cheaper that way. Also if you still have milk you can start sending about three packs so we can use it up. If you have gotten rid of it don't buy more. Everything else is going well. I'm getting closer to the half-way point which is at about 1,088 miles in Pennsylvania. I've been 812 miles up to today. I won't send a postcard so my next drop after Linden, Va., is Boiling Springs, PA 17007. ETA 6/23/1999. I miss you. Love, Joe."

Joe followed this note with another in four days.

"Wednesday, 6/2/1999 - Note to Mrs. Ward - Momma, I'm in Waynesboro, Va., staying at the YMCA. They let hikers camp here and use their shower. I just got in yesterday afternoon and I'll leave today. Just needed to pick up a few things, eat a good meal and get a shower. It's still cool at night but getting pretty warm during the day so I'm sweating a lot."

Right now things were going fine and dandy for Smoky Joe but he would soon engage the somewhat restrictive confines of the Shenandoah National Park - stomping grounds of the old Civil War general Stonewall Jackson. If things were a little unusual there it could be expected. Stonewall Jackson was a little unusual. He loved lemons as much as Smoky Joe loved ice cream!

Credits: Info of Joe Ward; Info of John David Harrell; Appalachian Trail info; Buck Nelson photo; personal notes; other sources.

Part 25
Smoky Joe's Location Marks Gen. Stonewall Jackson And Gen. John C. Breckinridge

Smoky Joe Ward, center, was surrounded by Civil War history as he passed through Waynesboro on the Appalachian Trail. General Stonewall Jackson, taught at the Virginia Military Institute (VMI) at Lexington and was later Gen. Lee's right-hand man. Moses Ezekiel , right, a cadet at VMI, fought at New Market with the 257 strong cadet body who responded to the call of General John C. Breckinridge. Ezekiel was later a famous sculptor and created a memorial at VMI. Breckinridge later hid out at Jacksonville, Ga., at the end of the war. [Photo credits: VMI]

Joe Ward was reviewing his journal and catching up on recording his data:

"Monday, 5/31/1999 - Day 69 - 15.3 miles today, 827.2 total, average 11.99."

"Tuesday, 6/1/1999 - Day 70 - 11.6 miles today, 838.8 total, average 11.98."

As time consuming and regular as it was the keeping of a journal was important to Joe. He needed to stay on task and the numbers in the journal prompted him ahead. The math told the story and if he lagged behind his average would drop and that would mean more days on The Trail. Joe knew he had to make sufficient progress to make his plan work.

"Wednesday, 6/2/1999 - Day 71 - 0 miles today, 838.8 total, average 11.81. Got carried away at the outfitter's and spent a lot of money. Got some things I needed and some I just wanted. Got a new backpack that's a little smaller and fits me a lot better. Should make hiking more enjoyable. Also got a lightweight summer sleeping bag, a new cartridge for my water filter. Bought several other things. I've really got to watch my money now. It was so late after I finished at the outfitter that I decided to stay another day and get my new pack organized. This was my first "0" day (no walking) since I started."

In addition to the trail math Smoky Joe Ward of Jacksonville, Ga., was contending with income tax concerns and other business items while out on the Appalachian Trail. No matter where you go the income tax forms have to be done. Fortunately for Joe he was getting a refund. In fact, his mother seemed to have found him extra money from some source and this came as a surprise to Joe:

"I got your letter about my $142.00 tax refund and the 772.19 from Run To Win, but I didn't understand the deposit slip from the Merchant & Citizens Bank for $1772.19. Whatever you did was fine but maybe you can explain it in another letter. I go into the Shenandoah National Park today and will soon be out of Virginia. Love, Joe."

Joe was finding that his trek through the mountains was quite expensive. He seems to be telling us that if we plan to hike The Trail we should do our research and plan carefully.

"Thursday, 6/3/1999 - Note to Mrs. Ward - Momma, I'm in Waynesboro, Va. A little north of Tyro. I came into town to get some things from an outfitter. I bought much more than I intended to, so I'll be sending some of my old stuff home. Wanted to let you know so you wouldn't wonder why I sent so much. I spent about $500.00 on a new

pack, a lightweight summer sleeping bag, a new water filter and a few other things. I also sent some of my heavier clothes home. I'll need some of this back later. I thought I had planned this trip pretty well, but I'm finding out the hard and expensive way that I didn't do too well. Don't worry about my credit card bill. I'll take care of it somehow when I get home. Love, Joe."

Joe was glad to get away from the place where he had spent so much money. But the realization that this trip was expensive came again to Joe as he looked down at his footwear:

"Thursday, 6/3/1999 - Day 72 - 7 miles today, 845.8 total, average 11.75. Only seven miles out of town today to the first shelter in the Shenandoah National Park. Got to get back on track and get my average back up. Going to need new boots soon. These are coming apart. They have close to 1000 miles on them."

Smoky Joe was now in the territory of the old Civil War general Stonewall Jackson. Stonewall Jackson had taught at Virginia Military Institute (VMI) before going off to fight in the Civil War and said that VMI would make a name for itself in the war. He was speaking of its graduates. But on one occasion the cadets at VMI walked out of their classrooms and responded to General John Breckinridge's emergency at the Battle of New Market and many were wounded and some killed there. But the cadets, though very young, but very brave, won the battle. A monument is now located on that campus in their honor. Smoky Joe was now in this area. It is interesting to note that the commander of the cadets in this battle, General John C. Breckinridge, hid out in Jacksonville, Ga., for a couple of days after the war on his flight to freedom. The folks at Jacksonville, Ga., aided his escape. In fact, he rested in one of the beds in one of the homes there. The story of his flight through Jacksonville, Ga., is told in previous articles of this series.

But Smoky Joe was having a battle of his own, and like the fighting cadets at New Market whose shoes and boots were literally sucked off by the deep mud, Joe was having a problem keeping his worn-out boots on his feet.

"Friday, 6/4/1999 - Day 73 - 13.1 miles today, 858.9 total, average 11.76. So far the Shenandoah Valley isn't that pretty and park regulations and scarce water make you stay in shelters like in the

Smokies. I don't like this because of the crowds. On a better note there are several stores and restaurants close to the trail. I'll hit one tomorrow."

Smoky Joe had now become accustomed to seeing some undesirable or bad things along The Trail but he knew if he looked hard enough he would see some of the good. And he sure would, at this point, like to think that those old bad boots on his feet would last until he could replace them with some new ones.

General Breckinridge hid at Jacksonville, Ga. after The Civil War

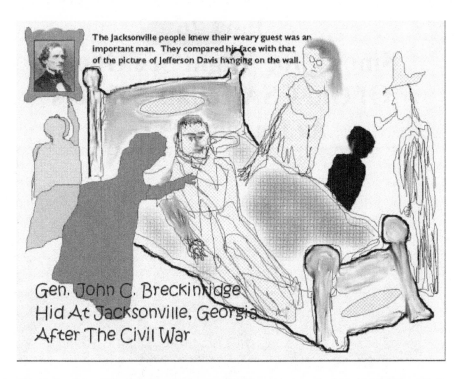

The Jacksonville people knew their weary guest was an important man. They compared his face with that of the picture of Jefferson Davis hanging on the wall.

Gen. John C. Breckinridge Hid At Jacksonville, Georgia After The Civil War

Credits: Info of Joe Ward; Info of John David Harrell; Appalachian Trail info; VMI info; Breckinridge notes; personal notes; other sources.

Part 26
Smoky Joe Might See Ghosts
Of Old CSA Telfair Soldiers
At Harpers Ferry

Smoky Joe Ward was now in the Shenandoah National Park. It was a place of beauty and history. The ground he walked over had been marched over by the troops of General Stonewall Jackson. And like the Civil War troops of Stonewall, Joe's boots were wearing out. And like Stonewall, he was trying to reach Harpers Ferry. [Photo credit: Shenandoah National Park]

Smoky Joe Ward looked at his worn-out boots and wondered if they would last until he got some new ones broken in. However, he did not even have the new boots in his possession but he hoped they would be coming soon. The Appalachian Trail exacted its toll on one's constitution and Smoky Joe was now seeing that the challenge was taking a lot out of him. Fortunately, the Shenandoahs weren't as hard on his feet as other places had been and he was grateful for that.

"Saturday, 6/5/1999 - Day 74 - 21.4 miles today, 880.3 total, average 11.89. Big day today (21.4 miles). The Shenandoahs aren't as tough as parts of the trail so maybe I can get my average back up. Went by a store and restaurant today for lunch. It was at a campground just off the skyline drive - a scenic road through the park. There should be several of these before I get out of the park. Been seeing a lot of deer lately and have taken some pictures."

Joe Ward had not caught a glimpse of the ghost of Civil War General Stonewall Jackson but Jackson and his troops had done a lot of walking around this area. So much they had gotten the nickname "foot cavalry." Stonewall often marched his troops around in circles and wound up in unexpected places - sometimes to the dismay of the Union army. Historians are still debating whether these tactics reflected brilliance on the part of Jackson or were the result of his unorthodox behavior. The old general was very eccentric and it is said he often went around with one arm raised because he either thought it longer than the other or that his body was not symmetrical. He also had the odd habit of eating lemons as he went into battle. It is said he was such a sleepyhead that he was sometimes lifted asleep into his saddle for yet another mysterious march.

Joe Ward could relate to the soldiers of Stonewall Jackson. He was now on their turf and he was feeling much like a member of the "foot cavalry." Like him, the old soldiers wore out many pairs of boots and were sometimes without footwear. This would soon be the case with Joe if his new boots didn't make a timely arrival. But he had some conveniences not available to the Civil War troopers.

"Sunday, 6/6/1999 - Day 75 - 12.6 miles today, 892.8 total, average 11.9. Stopped at another camp store today just off the trail. Bought some snacks for the next couple of days and ate a lot while I was there. Prices weren't too bad considering the location. So far the stores are the best part of the Shenandoahs. They also had a coin-operated shower ($1 for 5 minutes) and a washing machine. The next shelter north was only one mile so I'll go to bed clean tonight. I've put my tent up the last two nights in spite of regulation requiring you to stay in shelters. I like the tent much better if it's not raining. Haven't had any rain in a good while."

Joe could survive if he could just get to some ice cream. We see here that he found some:

"Monday, 6/7/1999 - Day 76 - 11.4 miles today, 904.2 total, average 11.89. Stopped at another store today and got some ice cream. I'm sitting outside the shelter now writing this and three deer are feeding right outside. They're almost tame. I called Cabela's today about my boots which are coming apart. They are going to replace them."

It is interesting to note how Joe was still sticking to his hiking plan. Author Bill Bryson had made a note of the progress of hikers on the Appalachian Trail. In one year 1,500 hikers had started the trail and 20 percent had dropped out before reaching Neels Gap in North Carolina. Only about a third of the hikers made it to Harpers Ferry (almost halfway) and just 300 reached the ultimate goal of Mt. Katahdin in Maine. Smoky Joe was feeling good because he was closing in on Harpers Ferry.

"Tuesday, 6/8/1999 - Day 77 - 15.1 miles today, 919.3 total, average 11.94. Eleven weeks on the trail. Another store today but I didn't eat this time. It was only a mile from the store to the shelter I was staying at so I cooked when I got to camp. Only one more night in the Shenandoah National Park and then I won't be passing so many stores. Also I won't be seeing so many people."

But like Stonewall Jackson, Smoky Joe Ward had his eye on Harpers Ferry, West Virginia. There the hauntingly beautiful place would conjure up the spirit of John Brown who was hanged there. John Brown had taken over the federal arsenal and the United States didn't take kindly to his actions. As fate would have it a young soldier named Robert E. Lee was sent there to subdue Brown. Stonewall Jackson was there to see him hanged. Later both Lee and Jackson would be fighting not for the United States but for the Confederacy. Another person was there for the hanging of John Brown - John Wilkes Booth. History has a strange way of developing.

But right about now the only thing Smoky Joe was developing was a way to get more ice cream and fewer black flies:

"Wednesday, 6/9/1999 - Day 78 - 13.1 miles today, 932.4 total, average 11.95. Another store today. It may be the last one in the park. Had a coke and some ice cream. Got to the shelter about 3:30 PM. No

one here yet but several are on the way It's getting pretty hot during the day and black flies are bad. So far no mosquito problem - too dry I guess."

But tomorrow would be another day. And Harpers Ferry was getting closer and closer. It would be a beautiful sight. And an important milestone in this long, long journey. And Joe might see some of the ghosts of the old Georgia 49th of Telfair, CSA. If he hears something like a bridge being wrecked it might be some of the old soldiers from Jacksonville, Georgia.

Credits: Info of Joe Ward; Info of John David Harrell; Appalachian Trail info; VMI info; "A Walk in the Woods" by Bill Bryson; personal notes; other sources.

Part 27
Smoky Joe Arrives At Harpers Ferry And A Lot Of History

John Brown's Fort

John Brown

Harpers Ferry

Smoky Joe Ward

Appalachian Trail hiker Smoky Joe Ward of Jacksonville, Ga., was now reaching Harpers Ferry, West Virginia. Soon he would mark his 1,000 mile mark on The Trail. Harpers Ferry had a lot of history. Abolitionist John Brown took over the federal arsenal there and held some 60 villagers hostage. The United States Government sent a young officer by the name of Robert E. Lee to flush him out. Brown was tried and hanged. But Brown's prophecy proved accurate. The issue of slavery had to be resolved. Ironically, here at Harpers Ferry a record number of Federal troops were captured by General Stonewall Jackson during the Civil War - some 12,500. [Photo credit: Harpers Ferry National Park Archives]

Black flies! The little pests were about as much as Smoky Joe

Ward could take with all the other things he had to be seeing about. Maybe as he got nearer that fabled place of Harpers Ferry, West Virginia, they would disappear. He hoped so. Maybe General Stonewall Jackson sucked on lemons to deter the ancestors of these same little creatures of the Shenandoahs during the Civil War. He was doing it for some reason. Joe thought again what a hassle it must have been for the soldiers of the Civil War to contend with all these elements and more. They certainly had their work cut out for them. Keeping shoes on your feet was a major undertaking. And he would be glad when the new boots arrived. He needed them; the old ones had about had it.

We can tell at this point that Joe is getting excited about getting to Harpers Ferry, West Virginia.

"Thursday, 6/10/1999 - Day 79 - 18.5 miles today, 950.9 total, average 12.04. Hit twelve miles a day average today. (Right On Schedule) I wanted to accomplish this by the halfway point. I need this average to do the whole trail in 180 days. Into Linden tomorrow for a food drop. 48.5 miles to Harpers Ferry, West Virginia and the 1,000 mile mark."

Smoky Joe knew his arrival at Harpers Ferry would, like Stonewall Jackson's capture of the place, be a high point in his endeavor. In his mind's eye he could see two great rivers come together at the bottom of the great mountains. At that very place would be the town of Harpers Ferry. Was the old armory really haunted by the ghost of John Brown who was hanged for taking over the federal arsenal? Did old John's ghost walk the streets at night and early morning? The place of Harpers Ferry had a lot of history. And a lot of hikers of the Appalachian Trail. Joe couldn't wait to mark that milestone.

And if you ever want to undertake that great challenge of the Appalachian Trail be sure to read Joe's words on the subject of food. He was finding out that he needed to eat more for the calories that furnished him the energy needed to do The Trail:

"Thursday, 6/10/1999 - Dear Momma, It's late afternoon and I've had supper and I'm ready to turn in at a shelter close to Linden, Virginia. I'll go in tomorrow morning for my food drop. I'm trying to eat cereal again with powdered milk so here are some changes for my next drops. Add four packs of powdered milk, three bags of rice (total seven) and three bags of Grape Nuts (total seven). Stop sending

oatmeal, hot chocolate, coffee, sugar and soap (hand and laundry). Everything else the same. I hope you still have the milk. I'm eating a lot more food now. All that you send plus I'm buying extra stuff in town. I don't believe I was eating enough for a while and my energy is better now. I'm even mixing M&M candy with my peanuts for extra calories."

And Joe was hoping, but in vain, that the new boots would beat him to Harpers Ferry and would be waiting for him there.

"The backpack that I sent home has some stuff in it that may need washing or airing out. My boots are just about worn out but Cabela's is going to send me a new pair to Harpers Ferry, West Virginia, because I've had them less than 90 days. They will charge them to me but give me credit on my Visa when I return the old ones. Check my statement and make sure they do. It may be awhile before I send the old ones back because I'll have to keep them both until I break the new ones in. By the time you get this letter I should have made it to Harpers Ferry, W. Va., and 1,000 miles .The next drop after Boiling Springs, Pennsylvania, is Port Clinton, PA 19549, ETA 7/1/1999. I'm not far from Boiling Springs so mail early. Thanks for everything. Love, Joe."

Smoky Joe was again looking forward to a "town break." He knew he must make the best of these relaxing moments because not too far in the future he would be in a no-man's-land where there would be no towns and no stores - not even roads.

"Friday, 6/11/1999 - Day 80 - 9.9 miles today, 960.8 total, average 12.01. Short day today. Into Linden, VA, for supplies Usually don't make too many miles on "town" days.

But more than anything at the moment the old Civil War magnet of Harpers Ferry was drawing Joe ever so strongly. Stonewall Jackson would have been proud of the perseverance of Smoky Joe Ward:

"Saturday, 6/12/1999 - Day 81 - 15.9 miles today, 976.7 total, average 12.05. Two more days to Harpers Ferry, West Virginia, and the 1,000 mile point."

Joe was focused on his mission. He had to remain focused. He was finding out along the way that former comrades on The Trail had given up and gone home. He must not let the thought enter his mind. But the aggravating jagged dangerous rocks of Pennsylvania ahead would not help matters. From what he had heard they were pure torture. But right now he had better things on his mind:

"Sunday, 6/13/1999 - Day 82 - 14.1 miles today, 990.8 total, average 12.08. Into Harpers Ferry, West Virginia, tomorrow. Only about nine miles. Camp at KOA campground with showers and laundry for $4.00. May split a motel room with another hiker if it's raining. (It's supposed to.)"

Smoky Joe had now gone farther than most Appalachian Trail hikers. Tomorrow he would go to the Appalachian Trail Headquarters and they would take his picture and register him, recording his progress since leaving Georgia. It was a good feeling. Smoky Joe was smiling. Things were looking good. He thought he would make it after all.

Credits: Info of Joe Ward; Info of John David Harrell; Appalachian Trail info; VMI info; personal notes; other sources.

Part 28
Half A Gallon Of Ice Cream And The Mason-Dixie Line

Smoky Joe Ward makes it to the half-way point of his hike of the Appalachian Trail. Here in Pennsylvania he stayed at the Iron Master's Hostel, formerly the Ironmaster's Mansion. The Ironmaster's Mansion, built in 1827, served as the residence for the ironmaster of Pine Grove Furnace Ironworks.The ironworks manufactured cannonballs during the Revolutionary War, and the hostel was a stop on the Underground Railroad for slaves seeking freedom. Joe was in the midst of history. [Photo and info credit: Pennsylvania Department of Conservation and Natural Resources]

Smoky Joe Ward was about to leave the South and enter the North. He knew now that his goal was in the cross-hairs of reality. Hiking the remainder of the entire Appalachian Trail was not going to be a piece of cake but he was determined to make it to Maine! He had come too far to quit. The Lord had blessed him on his journey and He was about to bless him again. As Joe looked heavenward and sniffed the air he could smell the freshness of rain. But right now he was headed for a motel room for another welcomed break. The rain would probably wait until he got on The Trail again.

"Monday, 6/14/1999 - Day 83 - 8.6 miles today, 999.4 total, average 12.04. Into Harpers Ferry, West Virginia, today. I'm sharing a room with another hiker. It was a good feeling to hit 1000 miles. I stopped at the ATC (Appalachian Trail Conference) headquarters on the way in and signed their register. They also took my picture for a photo album with the date I started in GEORGIA (March 24), etc. I was number 280 or so to pass through Harpers Ferry."

On Monday, 6/14/1999, Joe wrote his mother and Johnny Harrell, his hike coordinator, about his current status, the picture taking and the fact he was getting to stay at a motel again.

"When I leave in the morning and cross the river I'll be in Maryland. Only forty miles in Maryland and then into Pennsylvania. Joe."

Joe must have thought of the legend of George Washington tossing a coin across the Potomac River as he crossed that great stream. The Father of Our Country must have had a good arm to do that!

"Tuesday, 6/15/1999 - Day 84 - 16 miles today, 1015.4 total, average 12.08. Left Harpers Ferry about 11:00 AM, crossed the Potomac River and hiked into Maryland. I'm still hiking with "Pots", the hiker I split a room with and have been hiking with off and on for awhile. A couple from Canada, "Ma and Pa" who I've also been with left the trail to go to Washington for a few days."

Smoky Joe Ward seemed to enjoy the variety of people he found on The Trail. They all had something in common - much determination! But all were different and Joe enjoyed being with these characters called hikers of the Appalachian Trail. But you might see one today and not see him again for awhile - or ever again! That's just the way it is on the Appalachian Trail.

"Wednesday, 6/16/1999 - Day 85 - 15.2 miles today, 1030.6 total, average 12.12."

Joe had no comment for today except for the recording of his statistics. Part of it was because he was busy handling that expected rain that had now come to The Trail.

"Thursday, 6/17/1999 - 14.2 miles today, 1044.8 total, average

12.15. Rained last night and off and on most of the day. First rain in a long time. I got my tent up before it started and took it down during a letup this morning so it wasn't too bad. Some springs were starting to dry up so it was needed. It wasn't bad hiking in the rain and I stayed cool. I'm in Yankee territory now. I left Maryland today and crossed the Mason-Dixon line into Pennsylvania. 33.2 miles to the half-way point and half-gallon of ice cream. I stopped short of where I had planned to go today to make sure I got in a shelter to dry out. It's 6:30 PM and so far I'm here by myself."

Joe liked ice cream but he didn't know if he was up to half of a gallon! He would just have to see when he got to the store that had it.

"Friday, 6/18/1999 - Day 87 - 15.9 miles today, 1060.7 total, average 12.19. Cool this morning - in the upper 40's. Sleeping bag felt really good. Hiked into South Mountain, PA, to a store. It was two and a half miles round trip. So far the rocks in Pennsylvania haven't been any worse than what I've already seen. They're supposed to get pretty bad. I hope to make the half-way point tomorrow."

Joe wanted to be cautious about those Pennsylvania rocks. He had heard of hikers who ended their hike on account of severe injuries received as a result of falling on the rocks. He didn't want to become a casualty. Even the Civil War combatants had to battle those Pennsylvania rocks over at Gettysburg. Joe knew he had to watch those rocks. They were dangerous.

"Saturday, 6/19/1999 - Day 88 - 17.3 miles today, 1078 total, average 12.25. Into Pine Grove State Park just south of half-way point and at the general store where I was supposed to eat a half-gallon of ice cream to mark the half-way point. I've been going into so many stores and eating ice cream lately that I wasn't in the mood for a half-gallon so I had a pint. I spent the night in the Iron Master's Hostel. An old mansion built in the 1820's that was once used by the underground railroad for slaves trying to get north."

As Joe relaxed at the hostel that night he could almost hear the excited voices of the people who were escaping from bondage and looking forward to a better life. He thought about what a hard time they probably had in getting enough food along the way. And there he was eating ice cream. But there had been ice cream back in the old days prior to the Civil War. In fact, one Jacob Fussell is said to have produced the first commercial ice cream plant in 1851. Wonder if he was related to the Jacob Fussells of Jacksonville, Georgia?

But the ice cream was getting to him and Joe dozed off in peaceful slumber. He would need the energy of the ice cream come tomorrow. And he would need to dodge those dangerous Pennsylvania rocks!

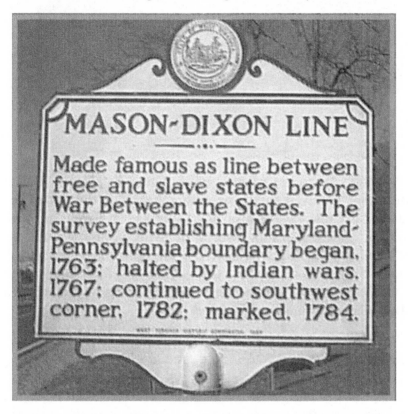

Credits: Info of Joe Ward; Info of John David Harrell; Appalachian Trail info; personal notes; other sources.

Part 29
Amish Country, Bad Rocks And Wanting New Boots

Smoky Joe Ward of Jacksonville, Ga., had now hiked to Duncannon, Pennsylvania. The Susquehanna River added to the beauty of the place. Joe also met some Amish people up around that area. The Amish folk seem to be living in the past and in the slow lane but they might be experiencing some of the things we are missing. Smoky Joe also started getting his first taste of those famous Pennsylvania Rocks. They weren't going to be fun. [Photo credits: Kenneth Pugh and *jackdied.com*]

Joe Ward thought about his native Ocmulgee River swamp around Jacksonville, Georgia, as he looked around his present surroundings. He was enjoying Pennsylvania more and more and the beauty of the place appealed to him. Also, he again had company and it meant a lot to have someone to talk with. He was also making more daily miles and upping his average.

"Sunday, 6/20/1999 - Day 89 - 19.1 miles today, 1097.1 total, average 12.32. Got to the half-way marker at 8:45 AM. Took some pictures of me and one with another hiker (L H "51") from Pennsylvania. We have hiked together off and on for awhile. He's about my age. He cooked pancakes for us at the hostel before we left this morning.Pennsylvania still isn't as rocky as I've heard and is pretty country. The woods are more open than Virginia. It's almost like the river swamp at home but has different kinds of trees and there are ferns

instead of palmettos."

At this time Joe must be avoiding the red bugs if there's any up that way. They have a way of getting a fellow's attention and encouraging him to make comments about their presence. Evidently they weren't biting Joe. Maybe he left those in the Ocmulgee River swamp. Right now his feet were still wishing for new boots. And he was almost in New York.

"Monday, 6/21/1999 - Hey, got into Boiling Springs today for food drop. My new boots still haven't come so I'll forward them on. It's raining again today. Next drop after Port Clinton, Pennsylvania, is Unionville, N.Y. 10988. ETA 7/8/1999. Joe."

"Monday, 6/21/1999 - Day 90 - 12.6 miles today, 1109.7 total, average 12.33. Out of Boiling Springs, PA, today about 10:00 AM. Didn't make it to first shelter so I decided to camp early."

Pennsylvania rocks! Maybe worse than the Broxton Rocks just south of Jacksonville, Georgia. Right about now, Smoky Joe is beginning to see the heralded possibility of bad rocks in the commonwealth. These rocks would probably finish off the old boots for good. Now is not the time to get stranded barefoot!

"Tuesday, 6/22/1999 - Day 91 - 14.6 miles today, 1124.3 total, average 12.35. Camping on the Susquehanna River at a fishing camp - $3.50 for tent space and shower. The trail came right through Duncannon, PA, today just before this fish camp. I feel like a hobo walking down the sidewalk with my pack and beard and dirty clothes. The rocks are supposed to get bad from here on across Pennsylvania. I got a little taste of them today."

Joe doesn't mention red bugs but lets us know there are the famous, fearsome and ubiquitous mosquitoes up that way, too:

"It's 7:30 PM and I've had my macaroni and cheese. The mosquitoes are buzzing so I had better get my $3.50 shower and get in the tent. I'll go by a truck stop just off the trail for breakfast. I think I'm finally eating enough and may have gained a little weight back. My energy is better now."

I wondered if Joe would see any Amish folks up there in Pennsylvania. He did:

"Wednesday, 6/23/1999 - Day 92 - 12.7 miles today, 1137 total, average 12.36. Had a big breakfast at the truck stop on my way out of town. There was a big bunch of Amish men, women, and children eating. They were dressed in the traditional Amish style and all seemed to be relaxed and enjoying themselves. I took some pictures of the Susquehanna River as I crossed and from the mountain on the other side."

Joe was now in for a big surprise. He actually met a hiker on The Trail who had hiked all the way from The Keys in Florida, to the beginning of The Trail at Springer Mountain, Ga. On his journey he had come through Joe's hometown of Jacksonville, Georgia.

"Thursday, 6/24/1999 - Day 93 - 14.9 miles today, 1151.9 total, average 12.38. Met a boy (Scotty) who started hiking in the Florida Keys and hiked all the way to Springer Mountain. He came through Jacksonville (Georgia) on 441 and he is going all the way to some part of Canada. He has someone following him a motor home so he doesn't have to carry a pack. His motor home was at a road where the trail crossed so I got to talk to him and his driver. They gave me a Pepsi and the most unusual sandwich I ever had. It had bologna, peanut butter, pickles and lettuce. It was pretty good."

Now, if Smoky Joe could survive that sandwich he could survive about anything. But you aren't too choosy on The Trail. Just about any kind of food tastes good. Joe made a mental note of his surroundings. The rocks were getting more numerous and the people were thinning out:

"Friday, 6/25/1999 - Day 94 - 12.7 miles today, 1164.6 total, average 12.39. Over half-way through Pennsylvania now. It is getting rocky, but so far not as bad as I expected. I've been skipping shelters and using my tent more lately. It's nice when it's not raining. I'm seeing less people now."

Joe looked sadly at his boots. How much more could they take? How much longer could they last? But, look at the bright side. At least the red bugs weren't biting.

Credits: Info of Joe Ward; Info of John David Harrell; Appalachian Trail info; *jackdied.com* for photo of Amish; personal notes; other sources.

Part 30
Fellow Hiker Fell And Hit Her Head – Required 25 Stitches!

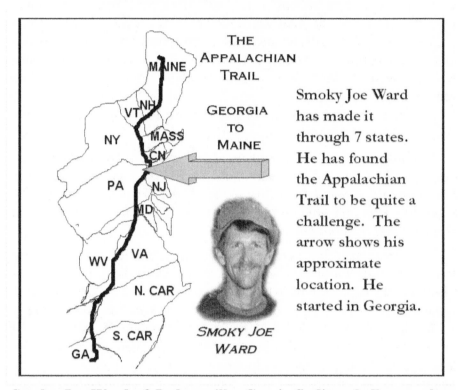

THE APPALACHIAN TRAIL

GEORGIA TO MAINE

Smoky Joe Ward has made it through 7 states. He has found the Appalachian Trail to be quite a challenge. The arrow shows his approximate location. He started in Georgia.

SMOKY JOE WARD

Smoky Joe Ward of Jacksonville, Ga., is finding challenges along the Appalachian Trail. Pennsylvania has plenty of sharp hard rocks but is a little short on water. Hopefully Joe is getting out of the rocks and maybe there will be better water supplies ahead. He would like to spend the Fourth of July in a cool water hole.

Smoky Joe Ward looked forward to his birthday as he trudged along The Trail that Saturday. He probably never thought he would be celebrating his birthday on the Appalachian Trail.

"Saturday, 6/26/1999 - Day 95 - 14.7 miles today, 1179.3 total, average 12.41."

"Sunday, 6/27/1999 - Day 96 - 13.1 miles today, 1179.3 total, average 12.42."

Port Clinton, Pennsylvania, was waiting for Joe and his arrival on Sunday. He arrived in town about 4:00 PM and was disappointed that the Port Clinton Hotel was full. But his trail buddies came along and helped him celebrate his birthday. "Pete" from New York even bought Joe a shower for $5.00. That was a nice present because showers are at a premium on the Appalachian Trail. Thru-hikers know how to value this precious privilege. After his shower Smoky Joe camped at the town pavilion for free. Maybe it wasn't so bad after all that the hotel had no vacancy.

Joe was about to get some of that rain we would love to see down our way today. It would cost him a few miles:

"Monday, 6/28/1999 - Day 97 - 6.1 miles today, 1198.5 total, average 12.36. Out of town about 12:30 PM after getting food drop from post office. I only went 6.1 miles to the first shelter because it looks like rain. It's thundering as I write this. I hope to be out of Pennsylvania in about one week."

The break gave Joe a chance to write home and tell his mother and Johnny Harrell, his hike coordinator, about his birthday party at Port Clinton and the nice shower he had. He told them at this stop he also had a chance to wash his clothes by hand. They were hanging out to dry at the moment. He added that he had only about 75 miles left of Pennsylvania. He would also be out of those treacherous Pennsylvania rocks! Kent, Connecticut, was looming ahead and had a nice ring to it. There he would receive his next food drop. He estimated he would arrive there on 7/15/1999. But before Connecticut would be New Jersey and New York. He needed to concentrate on getting through those states now.

Joe smiled as he gazed ahead for New Jersey, New York, Connecticut, Massachusetts, Vermont, New Hampshire, and Maine. He had already gone through Georgia, North Carolina, Tennessee, Virginia, West Virginia, Maryland, and now was completing Pennsylvania. He was making progress. Fourteen states in all and he had crossed the lines of seven of them. Seven down and seven to go!

Joe got back to the job of getting his miles back up to a respectable level:

"Tuesday, 6/29/1999 - Day 98 - 16.5 miles today, 1215 total, average 12.39."

Although Joe was getting some rain he saw that more was needed to keep the springs from drying up.

"Wednesday, 6/30/1999 - Day 99 - 16.8 miles today, 1231.8 total, average 12.44. We had a little rain the last two days but it is still very dry and a lot of springs are drying up. Water is getting to be a problem. It's there but I have to go farther down to get it and I have to carry more."

But Joe was not out of the Pennsylvania rocks yet! They were taking their toll and we find by his report that they were extremely dangerous:

"Thursday, 7/1/1999 - Day 100 - 16.7 miles today, 1248.5 total, average 12.48. 16.7 miles today between water sources. I had to carry a lot of extra water. Tomorrow will be about the same. Hopefully the water situation will get better in New Jersey. I haven't said much about the rocks lately because I haven't had anything good to say. They have really been bad. I don't really walk but just stumble along trying not to trip and fall. Several people have fallen and gotten scraped and bruised. "Sky Dog" fell and hit her head requiring 25 stitches."

Joe was not enjoying the water shortage and he was ready for a shower and looked forward to his next stop:

"Friday, 7/2/1999 - Day 101 - 13.9 miles today, 1262.4 total, average 12.50. Just six miles tomorrow and I'll be at the Pennsylvania-New Jersey state line and the rocks will supposedly start getting better. There's a church hostel in Delaware Water Gap and I plan to stay there Saturday and Sunday nights. I feel like a break will do me good and Sunday is the Fourth (July 4th) anyway. The hostel is free 'Donations'. There's been so little water lately that it's been hard to bathe off or wash out anything so I'm ready for a shower."

Despite the water shortage Joe could still see the beautiful sparkling mountain streams in his mind's eye. Actually they served as nature's air conditioner. They drew their coolness from the shade of the trees, mountain springs, and winter snows. And they returned the coolness to everything and everybody around them. Joe looked forward to finding a good cool hole and jumping in. There would be one ahead.

Julian Anderson Williams

A good way to celebrate the Fourth of July! Almost as good as being back in Jacksonville, Georgia.

A Fellow Could Get His/Her Head Hurt Real Easy In That Rock Pile

Credits: Info of Joe Ward; Info of John David Harrell; Appalachian Trail info; personal notes; other sources.

Part 31
Four Hamburgers, Cold Pond And Big Bear Brought A Memorable July Celebration

Smoky
and
The
Bear

SMOKY JOE
WARD

Smoky Joe Ward was making good progress on the Appalachian Trail. Not many things slowed him down. Maybe a good shower, a hamburger supper, or a good swimming hole. Or, maybe even a bear. But Smoky Joe and The Bear didn't take too much time to get acquainted. [Photo credit: Bear Image by David Kirshner & Frank Knight]

Joe looked forward to a cool refreshing shower. But Smoky Joe Ward knew there were hot days ahead and maybe few chances for more baths or showers. But at least he was about out of these Pennsylvania rocks. Whoever said they were bad was right on the money. Joe had barely escaped taking falls not missed by less lucky companions on The Trail. But they were tough travelers. They got stitches to close their wounds and moved on. That was the only thing to do. Joe glanced up at the hot sun one more time. A swimming hole would sure be a good way to celebrate The Fourth of July.

"Saturday, 7/3/1999 - Day 102 - 6.3 miles today, 1268.7 total, average 12.43. Into Delaware Water Gap this morning about 10:30. The church hostel was full so I've camped on the back lawn."

Joe liked one thing about the place. He was going to get that shower and he was going to need it because the weather was very hot. Still he wanted to press on:

"It's 2:00 PM and I've had a shower in the hostel and washed out some clothes by hand. There's no laundry in town. I've got my clothes hanging in the sun and waiting for it to cool off before I go to a store to get a few things. I think I'll leave in the morning instead of staying two days."

When Joe got a chance he would write home. It made the folks back there feel better and it gave him a sense of communicating with someone even if they were hundreds of miles away. If you are away from home for awhile it seems good to get mail. Joe looked forward to the post office stops. It made the wilderness a little more bearable.

"Sunday, 7/4/1999 - Card - Momma and Johnny, Camped here behind a church last night. I'm about ready to leave. I'll cross the Delaware River and be in New Jersey. Only about 900 miles to go. Joe."

But a good swim in a cool hole of water was still uppermost in Joe's mind. The heat had built up between his pack and his back and his comfort zone had about run out of space. He needed relief and hoped it would not be too long coming. Joe knew this recreation would trim his time and distance but he needed to be refreshed. He knew cold water immersion would do wonders for him and would be beneficial in the long run.

"Sunday, 7/4/1999 - Day 103 - 10.3 miles today, 1279 total, average 12.41. I left town just before noon and it was very hot. The bridge over the Delaware River was about ¾ of a mile long but had a

separate sidewalk. I didn't see a New Jersey state line sign for a picture. I hiked about 6 miles to "Sunfish Pond", a 40-acre clear, cold lake and jumped in to cool off. I'm camping at the Mohican Outdoor Center with another lake to swim in and a free shower. Since it was The Fourth the people at the center were cooking hot dogs and hamburgers for through hikers. I had two cokes and four hamburgers in about ten minutes."

I think at this point Joe has about convinced us that he is not bashful about pleasing his palate and supplying his stomach. Of course, his argument is very valid. The food tastes good because it has been only on rare occasions that he could partake of such civilized fare. Secondly, it is imperative that he maintain his energy level. So Joe had no hesitation about chow call. Joe had celebrated quite a few Fourths of July in his time but this one was a little special.

"It's about 7:45 PM now and I've hiked about half mile up to a ridge top with three other hikers to watch the fireworks in the valley from a nearby town. When I get back to camp I'll have that shower. The fireworks didn't start until about 9:30 PM and were very pretty. I didn't think to take my head light with me up the mountain so I had to try to see by other people's light coming down. It was almost midnight when we got down and we went for a swim instead of a shower. It was a good Fourth of July."

Now, Smoky Joe Ward had been pretty lucky up to this point concerning bears. He had seen no bears. But that was about to change. After all, the Appalachian Trail endeavor would not have been complete without the presence of a bear. But, first the bugs.

"Monday, 7/5/1999 - Day 104 - 14.3 miles today, 1293.3, average 12.43. It's been a long, hot day today and the mosquitoes and yellow flies are getting bad."

"Tuesday, 7/6/1999 - Day 105 - 9.4 miles today, 1302.7 total, average 12.40. I was camped with several other hikers last night. Just at dark we were pretty sure there was a bear walking around the camp. It sounded pretty big and loud. Several people have seen bears lately. "Medium Rare's" (dog) started barking and he said it only barks at bears and cows."

I suppose if the name "Medium Rare" would not attract a bear, nothing would. At least he had a dog that had all this animal identification business narrowed down to bears or cows. Of course, there was some significant differences in those two species and I don't really know if it helped matters much that the dog had that particular ability. In fact, it could be downright dangerous to have that dog around!

Joe continues:

"It must have been a bear last night because I saw one this morning just before leaving camp (my first one). It was a pretty big one (I'd guess about 200 lbs.) And it was coming down a ridge toward me, about 25 or 30 yards away. I heard it and stopped and we looked at each other for about a second; then it ran back over the ridge and out of sight."

Now, I can tell from the above narrative that Smoky Joe Ward is a far more ardent admirer of wildlife than I could ever claim to be. I would have tried to make the gap between the bear and me a little more than 30 yards and I would have stopped only if the bear had caught me. Hopefully, I would have been the one disappearing over the ridge and out of sight. My hat is off to Joe for not winding up "medium rare"!

Credits: Info of Joe Ward; Info of John David Harrell; Appalachian Trail info; personal notes; other sources.

Part 32

New York Trail Was Civilized But The City Was A Picture Of Chaos

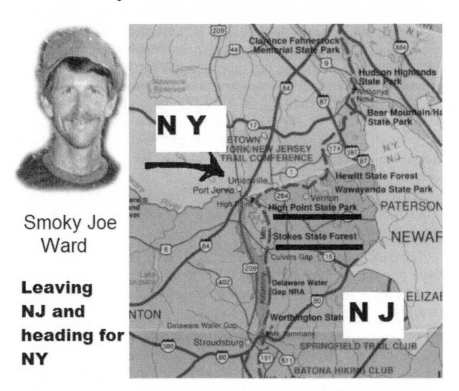

Smoky Joe Ward

Leaving NJ and heading for NY

Smoky Joe Ward of Jacksonville, Ga., survived his encounter with the big bear in New Jersey. He was now headed for New York and at one point could see the skyline of New York City. He smiled at the irony of being in the wilderness of civil order while in his view, in the distance, was the social and economic chaos of New York City. [Photo credit: Appalachian Trail source]

The big bear and Smoky Joe Ward looked at each other for what probably seemed an eternity to Joe. As his eyes got bigger and were glued to the view of the big creature in front of him he could hardly imagine how folks tracked these titans for food! Yes, even recently he had heard of a recipe for braised bear steak! He hated to think of some of the ingredients as the bear eyed him - flour, salt and pepper, cup of sliced onions, bacon fat, 3-inch slice of bear steak, cup of red wine, and some small forgotten amount of tomato paste. As he thought of the preparation of the ingredients - pound the flour into the steak with a meat pounder - he began to think the bear might be reading his mind. As his skin became a little more than clammy Joe thought of the irony of his situation. The bear might be thinking of preparing him for food! Joe's hiking buddy's nickname didn't help things, either - "Medium rare"! But the drama did not last much longer. The bear made his move. Fortunately, it was a quick turn and away he went over the nearest ridge. Joe had missed his bear steak but he really didn't have the appetite for such right now. This moment of the departed bear was one of great relief. The nearest thing similar to this was a retreat of a big wild boar hog in the swamp of the Ocmulgee River near Jacksonville, Georgia.

As Joe regained his composure and strength he thought about, of all things, eating something. But it would be his favorite - ice cream, not bear steak.

"Hitched a ride into Branchville, N.J., today (1.5 miles) to a Dairy Queen for an ice cream blizzard. Camped on a ridge top tonight. There's a little breeze so it's not as hot and the bugs aren't as bad as last night."

The hot weather continued to push Joe toward water. This country was famous for its cool clear lakes and streams and those made excellent swimming holes. Joe looked forward to getting to the beautiful state park that lay just ahead:

"Wednesday, 7/7/1999 - Day 106 - 10.3 miles today, 1313 total, average 12.38. The trail passed through High Point State Park today. The highest elevation in N.J. (1803 feet). I went swimming in a lake (free) and had two hot dogs, fries and a coke ($9.45). The food in my pack is about gone or I would not have paid that. I've been taking a few short days because it's so hot."

In all this wilderness beauty it had not occurred to Joe that he was near the great metropolis of New York City! There the population was huge and the pace much faster. Two worlds were here with a haze of separation between them. The irony of it all struck Joe. Here he was in the peace and quiet and civilization of the wild. Out there not too far was the not-so-civil wild, noisy and crazy life of New York City. He smiled. He was in the best place.

"Thursday, 7/8/1999 - Day 107 - 12.3 miles today, 1325.3 total, average 12.38. I didn't realize how close I am to New York City. I think I'm only about an hour's drive away. Into Unionville, N.Y., for food today. Nice little town, only .4 of a mile off the trail. I got my mail and had a good lunch. I hiked about five miles out of town to camp."

Joe was mentally preparing himself for the miles ahead. He knew the one hundred miles of pure wilderness lay ahead. The long stretch with no stores or anything else much for that matter. He knew there would be streams to cross with little help or no help from bridges or boats. He knew there would be severe weather and terrain. He wanted to be ready. He thought about his energy and knew sweet candy was a key player in his energy levels.

"Thursday, 7/8/1999 - Note to Mrs. Ward - I'm in Unionville, N.Y. I just got my package and sorted it out. Everything is fine. I asked Johnny on the phone today to add about a pound of plain M&M's candy to each package. I had a good lunch here and I'm resting a bit before heading back out. Love, Joe."

Joe continued to gauge his resources and supplies. He also wanted to travel as light as possible.

"Friday, 7/9/1999 - Day 108 - 12.8 miles today, 1338.1 total, average 12.38. Nice day today and it's cooled off some. I passed a store about 11:00 AM with homemade ice cream, fresh baked cakes, pies, fresh fruit, etc. I only had ice cream and some bananas. I ate more out of my food bag to save money and get the weight off my pack. Camped tonight near a state park office with running water."

As Smoky Joe passed from the beauty and ease of the New Jersey section of The Trail over into the New York section he knew things would be getting a bit tougher. And this was only the lower end of the gradual and escalating measure of a man's will to conquer The Trail. Ahead lay the more rigorous exercises of endurance and caution - New Hampshire and Maine.

"Saturday, 7/10/1999 - Day 109 - 12 miles today, 1350.1 total, average 12.38. I crossed the New York state line this morning. New

Jersey was nice with farm land, open fields and a lot of old stone walls. There were no rocks like Pennsylvania, at least not as many. The first few miles in N.Y. were a little tough scrambling over big rocks on a ridge top. It started raining during the night last night and I didn't have the rain fly on my tent. I woke up with rain hitting me in the face. I managed to get out and put it on before everything got too wet. I stopped during the day and dried everything out. I had more rain later in the afternoon while hiking but it felt good."

From his new vantage point Smoky Joe could see the skyline of New York City.

"Sunday, 7/11/1999 - Day 110 - 11.6 miles today, 1361.7 total, average 12.37. Cool this morning, in the upper 50's. My sleeping bag felt good. I went over Mombasha High Point today and could see the New York City skyline. I took a picture but it may not show much. Passed another little Deli about noon and had coffee and doughnuts. I got a sub to take with me. So far N.Y. has had some tough climbs but they don't last long. I guess I need to stay in shape for New Hampshire and Maine. Water is still scarce. I was supposed to go by a small waterfall today but it was dry. I camped in Harriman State Park by a pretty lake."

As Joe looked at the pretty water in front of him he wondered if there would be water enough when he got to the one hundred miles of no-man's-land in Maine. Only time would tell.

Credits: Info of Joe Ward; Info of John David Harrell; Appalachian Trail info; personal notes; other sources.

Part 33

Smoky Joe Didn't Want To Leave The Friars – They Were Good Cooks!

SMOKY JOE WARD

Graymoor Franciscan Religious Retreat In New York State

Joe Enjoyed Visiting (And Eating) With The Friars There

Smoky Joe Ward of Jacksonville, Ga., was now in the state of New York. His lodging place tonight was the Graymoor Friary Franciscan Retreat. The friars, or monks, there treated Joe and other Appalachian hikers to a good supper and breakfast. Joe didn't much want to leave the nice place but he knew he had to press on. [Photo credit: Graymoor Friary.]

Smoky Joe Ward of Jacksonville, Georgia, had plenty of reason to be concerned about the big bear he met in New Jersey. After Joe had his encounter with the bear another hiker coming along sometime after Joe complained to authorities about a bear bothering him. Seems the hiker was trying to sleep and the bear came up and began biting his foot. Now I can sleep under about any conditions but I don't believe I could get much shut-eye with a big black bear trying to have lunch on one of my appendages.

But now Smoky Joe had left the bear country of New Jersey and was in the state of New York. What he had heard was proving true.

This section of The Trail was not so easy. But he was glad there were stores and motels along the way up in the Empire State. Today he would see the skyline of New York City in the hazy distance. Today he would find out that one of his trail buddies had given up the chase and quit The Trail. It only made Joe more determined. The last figures he had read said only about 20% of hikers who begin the challenge ever finish The Trail. He intended to be one of those who finished:

"Monday, 7/12/1999 - Day 111 - 12 miles today, 1373.7 total, average 12.37. Crossed the Palisades Interstate Parkway this afternoon. It goes into N.Y. City only thirty-four miles east. I had to walk down the road aways (.4 mile) to a visitors center to get water. All the water sources are drying up. I'll carry a gallon out of here for camping tonight and some for in the morning. I saw the N.Y. City skyline again today. I saw in a hiker register today that "Snail" from California decided to quit the trail. New York continues to be tough with a lot of steep ups and downs and not much flat ridge walking."

Joe decided he needed a break from the lean-to's called shelters and looked forward to finding a town with a motel. It didn't take long.

"Tuesday, 7/13/1999 - Day 112 - 5 miles today, 1378.7, average 12.30. I went into Fort Montgomery, N.Y., to get a few supplies. I decided to stay the night in a motel. It's been a while since I have. No laundromat so I've washed my clothes in the sink and hung them out. I hate to spend the money but a break does me good."

Sometimes when Joe reviewed his trail guides and other trail info he almost got the blues. Now, the latest research was showing The Trail might be a mite longer than 2,160 miles. The latest figure was 2,174. Joe wondered where the extra 14 miles came in. But the small difference was not going to make any difference to him. He was heading for Maine. He thought the better alternative tonight was to do a little trip planning. Anything for a helpful diversion. But soon he would be reminded of bears again.

"Wednesday, 7/14/1999 - Day 113 - 6.4 miles today, 1385.1 total, average 12.25. I'll cross the Hudson River on the Bear Mountain Bridge this morning just out of Fort Montgomery near West Point Military Academy. I was trying to roughly plan the rest of my trip last night. New Hampshire and Maine are going to be a challenge for

getting supplies. Maine has a hundred mile wilderness with no roads or stores. The Post Offices and other stores are also a long way off the trail. I had another short day because I wanted to stay at the Graymoor friary. This is a Franciscan religious retreat. They have a tenting area and let hikers eat supper and breakfast with them."

Joe knew after partaking of the fare that he made the right decision:

"Supper was really good with pasta and meatballs and homemade bread. They had a special table away from the others for hikers and they brought the food to us. There were about ten hikers. I'm looking forward to breakfast in the morning."

"Thursday, 7/15/1999 - Day 114 - 14.3 miles today, 1399.4 total, average 12.27. I had a good breakfast this morning. All you could eat of eggs, bacon, potatoes, coffee and juice."

The Graymoor Friary had helped many persons with alcohol problems. The rehabilitation center had also been friendly to Appalachian Trail hikers. This summer they were even extending hands of help to nearby nuns whose convent was being repaired. With the nuns staying in some of the facilities designated for hikers the hikers had to stay in temporary quarters on the grounds. But no matter. The food was still good and the folks there were mighty nice. There have been recent reports that the friary might have to close because of operational problems but that would be a shame. The place is a haven for folk who need help with their addiction problems. But, nice as it was, Smoky Joe had to press on:

"Friday, 7/16/1999 - Day 115 - 13.9 miles today, 1413.3 total, average 12.29. Into a little Deli/Store about .4 miles off the trail this afternoon. I had two cokes and some ice cream and I got sandwiches for tonight. I also got a few things to hold me till I get to Kent, Connecticut, Monday. There are a lot more stores close to the trail now than on the first part of my trip in Ga., N.C., Tenn., and Va. I think I'm gaining back the weight I lost initially. I'm just relaxing in the shade now. It's a little after 4:00 PM and I'm only going another four miles today. Tomorrow I pass by the train station that goes into New York City."

That night before leaving New York state Joe thought it might be a good idea to do a little catching up on his record-keeping. He knew this little task was important to him in many ways. It was a motivator and good records would mean a good journal. Who knows? It might even help others who would try to hike The Trail in the future.

"Saturday, 7/17/1999 - Day 116 - 16.6 miles today, 1429.9 total, average 12.32. Have neglected my log for a few days. I may be off on last couple of days with daily mileage but today should be accurate. Johnny's note - I tried to correct mileage. I think it's right."

It was always good to get help from home. The support of his hike coordinator at Jacksonville, Ga., John David Harrell, was encouraging.

Credits: Info of Joe Ward; Info of John David Harrell; Appalachian Trail info; personal notes; other sources.

Part 34
Rain, New Boots And Buying Mosquito Repellent In Massachusetts

SMOKY JOE WARD IN MASSACHUSETTS

Smoky Joe Ward, after crossing Connecticut, is now in Massachusetts. Things are looking up for Joe and he is in good spirits. However, the mosquitoes are about to take him over. But it's only fifty miles to Vermont and then on to New Hampshire and Maine. The end is getting nearer. [Photo credit: Trail Source]

Lost. Smoky Joe Ward of Jacksonville, Georgia, scratched his head and shook it. How could he be lost? He had just come this way on the way down to town. But these kinds of "turn-a-rounds" cost you a lot of time and aggravation. Joe found out more than once that a casual mental note was not always enough. He would have to be more careful about marking his entrances and exits to The Trail when he left it.

"Sunday, 7/18/1999 - Day 117 - 12.4 miles today, 1442.3 total, average 12.32. Camped about one mile outside of Kent, Conn. I left my pack and went into town about 6:00 PM with "Woodchuck" and "Pepper" - a young married couple I've hiked and camped with some before. They are from Texas. I washed clothes and we ate pizza. It was 10:00 PM before I started back to camp. They stayed in town. I had my headlight and could see the trail pretty good but I couldn't find the turn to my tent. I was about to give up and go back to town because it was

really dark and lightning but I decided to go a little farther. I found it
eventually just past where I was going to turn around."

Joe had his new boots now! They felt pretty good but he knew he
would have to break them in. That might not be as easy on The Trail
day in and day out as it would be at home where he took occasional
jaunts through the Ocmulgee River swamp near his home at
Jacksonville, Ga. And he was now seeing a lot more people than he saw
back in the swamp in Georgia.

"Monday, 7/19/1999 - Day 118 - 7.3 miles today, 1449.6 total,
average 12.28. Out of town about noon. It's hard to get things done. I
can't get away from people wanting to talk - other hikers and just
curious people. Rained hard on me this afternoon with my new boots
on. Maybe it will help break them in. It's dark now and not raining.
Maybe it's stopped for the night."

Joe was making good progress and felt good about it. He was now
meeting hikers headed in the opposite direction - going north to south
instead of south to north as he was doing. He could tell them one thing
- they had a long way to go! And they better watch those Pennsylvania
rocks and New Jersey bears. But the whole trail would not be that bad.

"Tuesday, 7/20/1999 - Day 119 - 10 miles today, 1459.6 total,
average 12.26. So far Connecticut is about like New York with short
steep climbs. New boots OK so far. I've been using moleskin on spots
that feel like they might blister. Seven hundred miles to go."

Joe was thinking about how his trip had been and how it was going
now. He really felt good. Life was treating him right - at least for the
moment.

"Wednesday, 7/21/1999 - Day 120 - 15.7 miles today, 1475.3 total,
average 12.29. Camped about 3/4 mile outside of town just beside the
highway that goes into town (Salisbury, Conn.). Walked into town about
6:00 PM. It's amazing how I can hike 15 miles with a 45-pound pack
and walking one and a half miles round trip seems like nothing. I'll go
back to camp and cook supper and come back again in the morning for
breakfast and a few supplies before hitting the trail. I'm writing this as I
am sitting in a nice, deserted town park with tables and chairs. Life is
good. I've been meeting a few south bounders the last few days. Most of
them left Maine the end of May and have a long way to go to Georgia.

Tomorrow I cross into Massachusetts."

Joe was up and at 'em the next morning and he was glad to be with friends again on The Trail.

"Thursday, 7/22/1999 - Day 121 - 14.2 miles today, 1489.5 total, average 12.30. Had breakfast, bought a few things and was out of town by 8:30 AM. Crossed into Mass. this morning. I had a few tough climbs. I'm camping with "Woodchuck" and "Pepper".

"Friday, 7/23/1999 - Day 122 - 13 miles today, 1502.5 total, average 12.31. Days are very hot now and mosquitoes are pretty bad but the water situation is better."

As Joe swatted another mosquito he realized he was about out of repellent. It would not do to let these little boogers get a toe-hold.

"Saturday, 7/24/1999 - Day 123 - 13 miles today, 1515.5, average 12.32. Hitched a ride into Great Barrington, Mass., today to buy mosquito repellent. I was about out and I forgot it the last time I was in town. I caught rides into and out of town (4 miles) very quickly. I was thinking that I was getting pretty good at this until I got back on the trail headed south and walked about a mile and then I realized my mistake. It's another very hot day and my clothes stay soaking wet all day. The mosquitoes are terrible. Not just at night but all day. I've been on The Trail four months now. Fifty more miles and I'll be in Vermont and then on to New Hampshire and Maine."

Smoky Joe smiled. He saw the end was getting nearer. But he also knew there were some pretty stiff challenges ahead.

Credits: Info of Joe Ward; Info of John David Harrell; Appalachian Trail info; personal notes; other sources.

Part 35
The Strange Inspirations Of Highest Mountain In Massachusetts

Smoky Joe Ward of Jacksonville, Ga., makes it to Mount Greylock in Massachusetts. It is the highest mountain in the state. Joe was to find that many famous people were associated with this mountain. Herman Melville thought the mountain looked like a big whale and was so inspired he wrote "Moby Dick." Evidently the mountain made people think of the ocean. So much that this lighthouse destined for Boston wound up here on top of the mountain. Joe wound up there, too. [Photo courtesy of Mt. Greylock State Reservation]

Well, the New Year 2006 is here and we will be back on the Appalachian Trail trying to get Smoky Joe Ward to Maine. When we took a detour for a few Governor John Clark articles we left Joe in Massachusetts and that's where we will pick him up today. You probably don't remember but he was having a time with those pesky mosquitoes. Almost thought he was back in the swamp at Jacksonville, Ga. But today it was getting a little better:

"Sunday, 7/25/1999 - Day 124 - 12.7 miles today, 1528.2 total, average 12.32. Not quite as hot today and for some reason the mosquitoes weren't quite as bad. I'm camping by a pretty body of water which I filtered water out of. I don't usually do this but it was listed as a water source so it should be OK. I'm not seeing as many people now and I'm camping alone more."

Smoky Joe had about decided it must rain all over the world - especially the world he lived in. This northern section of The Trail was no exception. It seemed to generate moisture just like the southern portion. And it was getting cooler:

"Monday, 7/26/1999 - Day 125 - 13 miles today, 1541.2 total, average 12.33. It's cooler today and easier hiking."

"Tuesday, 7/27/1999 - Day 126 - 12.3 miles today, 1553.5 total, average 12.32. It rained last night and I had to get up and put the rain fly over the front of the tent. Into Cheshire, Mass., for food package. Catholic Church lets hikers sleep on floor in church annex. Father Tom is a former thru hiker. He did it in sections. It took him two years."

Father Tom's walking The Trail made Joe think a lot about his own father, also a member of the clergy. Rev. Wade Ward loved to walk and Joe could not help thinking that his dad would be very successful in hiking The Trail. Wade Wentworth Ward had walked a lot of miles in his life and probably composed many sermons and lesson plans doing it. He had also taught school. But he had departed those walking trails of earth in 1981. Joe thought again how good it would be to have him along on the Appalachian Trail.

Joe could now sense the coolness of the air and he had a feeling it was going to get a lot cooler; in fact, he had received word that heavier clothing would shortly be in order so he wrote home for some:

"Tuesday, 7/27/1999 Card - Dear Momma and Johnny, My next food package after Killington, Vermont, will be Glencliff, New Hampshire. ETA 8/14/1999. That's only a week after Killington so mail it early. That's where it's recommended that you get your warmer clothes back, so I'll need: Slumber Jack sleeping bag with the stuff bag (not Redi bag), black rain pants, black stocking cap, black gloves,

green fleece jacket and blue long underwear. Thanks, we're getting close to the end. Joe."

Now, whether he realized it at the time or not, Joe was coming up on a very special mountain - Mt. Greylock. Mt. Greylock has another name - Saddleback Mountain. It was this mountain that inspired Herman Melville to write "Moby Dick." When he finished the great book he celebrated on the top of Mt. Greylock. Other famous people were also connected to the mystical mountain. Henry David Thoreau slept at the top one night and it got so cold he piled boards upon himself to survive the night. As Herman Melville thought the mountain reminded him of a great whale and others related the mountain to the ocean. So much that a lighthouse destined for the coast at Boston wound up on top of Mt. Greylock! The lighthouse became a war memorial and guided pilots flying over the treacherous mountain range at night. Other famous people apparently drew inspiration from the great mountain. Norman Rockwell lived nearby and so did Daniel Chester French, sculptor of the Lincoln Memorial. Smoky Joe was going to a famous place.

"Wednesday, 7/28/1999 - Day 127 - 7.7 miles today, 1561.2 total, average 12.29. Short day today. Hiked to Mt. Greylock, the highest peak in Massachusetts (3,491 feet) and to the Bascom Lodge. I got a bunkroom and shower for $22. All the hotels in this area are very expensive so this was a good deal. It had been awhile since my last shower. They have a six dollar breakfast, too. I go into Vermont tomorrow."

At this point Smoky Joe could use some food but found the prices prohibitive. He had another run of good luck though:

"Thursday, 7/29/1999 - Day 128 - 13.2 miles today, 1574.4 total, average 12.30. I didn't eat supper at the lodge last night because it was $12. I cooked outside on my stove. After supper one of the other boys staying in my room said they had a lot of pizza left over in the dining room. I went down and asked if I could buy some. They let me have all I wanted free. I'm learning to be a good bum. I got a late start this morning after a big breakfast at the lodge and waiting for some bad clouds and lightning to pass. I still got into a little rain late this afternoon. I made it into Vermont about 5:00 PM. I'm hiking with "Patches." We camped with "Woodchuck," "Pepper," "Hillbilly,"

"Carolina Kid," and "Heavy Pack."

In the flickering campfire Joe could see the shadowy figures across from him and the determination in the faces of these comrades. They were jovial and funmaking on the outside but deep in, he knew they were of his own mind. They meant, like himself, to conquer the Appalachian Trail. That was the bottom line.

Credits: Info of Joe Ward; Info of John David Harrell; Appalachian Trail info; Mt. Greylock State Reservation notes; personal notes; other sources.

Part 36
Vermont Moose Were Huge

Smoky Joe Ward of Jacksonville, Ga., was now in Vermont. He had heard a lot about the state's big moose. Some weighed over a thousand pounds. Maybe he would see one. But if he didn't he would see other things of interest and challenge. The Appalachian Trail hike of Smoky Joe was a continuing adventure.

Smoky Joe Ward was going to encounter some surprises as he began the last long leg of his Appalachian journey. But, on the other hand, some of it would be routine. However, the scenery never really got routine. He saw places and felt seasons that reminded him of home at Jacksonville, Ga. He knew that returning home to Jacksonville would be an adjustment in itself. He had been on The Trail so long. It was almost a part of him by now. But back to the practical points of the day. At least for right now plenty of water was available and that was a blessing.

"Friday, 7/30/1999 - Day 129 - 13.1 miles today, 1587.5 total, average 12.30. We had a big thunderstorm last night but the tent kept everything dry. I had to pack the tent up wet but I stop during the day to

dry it out. Water has been fairly plentiful in Vermont."

Joe's eyes widened and his heart beat a little faster as he heard his companions and others talk of "the moose of Vermont." These huge animals were the stuff of tall tales. Huge ones would wander out in the roads and cars would hit them. Bumper stickers warned people - "Brake For Moose - It Could Save Your Life." And for good reason: some of these leviathans of the forest weighed around 1,200 pounds. The animals were multiplying despite the fact that some folks like moose meat. They say it tastes like "sweet beef." Others abhor the idea of having a moose meal and try to get laws enacted to protect the big animals. Sometimes you can see them around sunrise or dusk. They are hard to see by the road because their coats are dark and their eyes don't reflect light as do the eyes of some other critters. But Joe wanted to see one if possible.

"Saturday, 7/31/1999 - Day 130 - 16.8 miles today, 1604.3 total, average 12.34. Someone saw a moose today and I saw some droppings. I believe I'll have a good chance of seeing one, especially in Maine. The males can weigh 1200 pounds. Didn't make it to the shelter I was going to today before it got dark so I'm not camped in a very good place but I have enough water."

But Joe's thoughts were soon to be diverted from the image of a huge moose clumsily stepping on his tent (with him in it) to a place called Stratton Mountain and Stratton Village. This must be some exclusive place, Joe thought. They had saunas, an indoor pool, tennis courts, cardiopulmonary therapy, racquet ball courts, tanning beds and a bunch of other stuff that called for big bucks. He had to laugh at all that effort aimed at folks' wallets and their exercise regimen. Why, they could just jump out on the Appalachian Trail and get all the exercise and fresh air they needed. But he wanted to see the place. Just for the record.

"Sunday, 8/1/1999 - Day 131 - 8 miles today, 1612.3 total, average 12.30. Got to the top of Stratton Mountain about noon. There's a trail that runs from there to a ski lift about 0.8 mile away. Thru hikers are allowed to ride free to Stratton Village below. The normal price is $12. I rode down with "Circuit Rider" and "Ulysses." "Circuit Rider" is a preacher. About 7:00 PM we rode the lift back to the top where there is a ski patrol shack. They let thru hikers sleep in it. There was a great

view from there and a beautiful sunset.   We had a good day. "Woodchuck", "Pepper", "Carolina Kid", and "Heavy Pack" stayed, too."

Smoky Joe Ward knew he would be seeing things to indicate that he was getting to some of the last milestones of his long trip. In fact, everything now seemed to be an object of closure. It was a feeling that the adventure was narrowing ever so much. It was sort of a bittersweet realization for Smoky Joe. One he had just as soon not dwell on. Right now he had to find/get some supplies. These practical chores could not be ignored.

"Monday, 8/2/1999 - Day 132 - 13.7 miles today, 1626 total, average 12.31. Hitched a ride into Manchester Center, Vermont (5.5 miles) to get some supplies. The Episcopal Church runs a hostel. Five dollars for a shower and sleeping on the floor. I had a good meal and will have breakfast in the morning and hit the trail."

But New Hampshire and Maine were tangible entities out there in front of him. And like it or not, Joe was about to see them in the distance.

"Tuesday, 8/3/1999 - Day 133 - 10.2 miles today, 1636.2 total, average 12.30. Left Manchester Center about 10:30 AM. On top of Bromley Mountain I could see Stratton Mountain where I stayed in the ski patrol shack two days ago. Also, supposedly, I could see New Hampshire and Maine."

And Smoky Joe couldn't help but wonder about the terrific wind he had heard of on a mountain he was approaching. In fact, it held the world's record for wind speed. A fellow could get blown away up there and never be found! Not a pleasant thought at all.

"Wednesday, 8/4/1999 - Day 134 - 14.3 miles today, 1650.5 total, average 12.31. Having some cool mornings and comfortable nights now. It seems like September at home. I read that the average summer time high on Mount Washington is 52 degrees. Also the highest on-land wind speed in the world was recorded there (231 MPH). It might be good thing that my pack is so heavy."

But the feared mountain was still a ways ahead of Smoky Joe. He would have some time to think about the challenge ahead of him. He could just picture himself frozen stiff and blown like a pretzel across the bleakness of the high tops of New Hampshire mountain ranges. But Smoky Joe had come too far to turn back. He sort of looked forward to the challenge. One thing about this trip - it wasn't the least bit dull.

Credits: Info of Joe Ward; Info of John David Harrell; Appalachian Trail info; Vermont and New Hampshire info; personal notes; other sources.

Part 37

Surprises Just Ahead At Dartmouth College

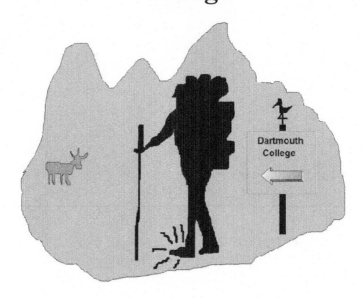

Smoky Joe Ward of Jacksonville, Ga., was almost to New Hampshire. Ahead lay terrible Mt. Washington where winds blew strong and fast enough at times to blow anything away. But right now he was contending with a very painful ankle. But there were surprises along the way to brighten the day. He thought he saw a moose but wasn't sure. He also wasn't sure he was hearing right when told of another surprise up the road at Dartmouth College. After all, he was just a country boy from Jacksonville, Ga.

Smoky Joe Ward kept looking ahead, wary as an old seasoned swamper of the not-too-far-away monster mountain called Washington. Not that he was afraid, but any place that could muster up a 231 mile-per-hour wind was a place due a little respect and fear.

But the caution mode was going to have to take a rest because Joe replaced his anxiety with pleasant palate-pleasing thoughts of the Whistle Stop Restaurant:

"Thursday, 8/5/1999 - Day 135 - 8.4 miles today, 1658.9 total, average 12.28. Another short day today. The Whistle Stop Restaurant was only a half mile off the trail and I couldn't pass it up. "Yogi", "Citrus", and "Thor" were there also. I had a burger, fries, banana split, and coffee. It rained while I was there, so that worked out good. I took a long break there and only had a mile and a quarter to where I'm camped. It's a pretty spot next to a stream. It's nice to be hiking and camping again after so many dry miles through the middle of the trail. It's windy and thundering now, like I may be in for a storm. I'm going to do some climbing tomorrow, back up to over 4000 feet."

Now with good food beneath his belt, Smoky Joe once again began thinking of closure points. He saw the end coming. He knew it had been a great adventure. And he knew he owed a lot to people close to him who had helped him make it happen.

"Friday, 8/6/1999 - Day 136 - 10.3 miles today, 1669.2 total, average 12.27. Less than 500 miles. I'll be in New Hampshire next week. A few months ago I thought I would never get there. Sooner than I realize I'll be climbing Mount Katahdin and this wonderful adventure will be over. Momma and Johnny, you will never realize what an important part you have had in this trip. I hope you have seen it as an adventure, too. This life on the trail has begun to seem so normal to me that there is going to have to be an adjustment period when I get home. My left ankle has been bothering me off and on for a good while. Today I turned it pretty badly. I've been worried about doing this for some time. I thought it was going to be serious but it seems to be doing OK. I've also noticed lately that when I sleep with my legs bent and wake up and try to straighten them out it takes a few seconds. I hope these legs and feet have 500 miles left in them."

Joe's words and tone seem now to project success for his endeavor. Now it was only a matter of time. Now the 231 MPH wind didn't figure into the equation. He was committed to the finish much more than he was to the start. It was something now that had to have the right conclusion. It could be no other way. The legs and feet would just have to last.

But, back to reality. Joe had basic things to take care of and they had to be taken care of now. A hiker wouldn't last long without nourishment.

"Saturday, 8/7/1999 - Day 137 - 5.4 miles today, 1674.6 total, average 12.22. Going into Killington, Vermont, for food drop. Got here about 10:00 AM. It's been slow going with my ankle still bothering me. There was a motel right beside the post office so I decided to stay for the night. There probably won't be too many more close to the trail and reasonably priced."

It wasn't hard for Smoky Joe to convince himself to stay another day in the motel. After all, it was Sunday. The perfect day to rest.

"Sunday, 8/8/1999 - Day 138 - 0 miles today, 1674.6 total, average 12.13. Raining this morning and forecast calls for it to continue all day. Decided to stay in motel another day. The rest will do me and my ankle good. Only the second day of the trip that I've done no hiking."

But the ankle was getting no better. In fact, it was getting worse. The future might have Joe saying, "I would have made it but the ankle went out." The pain was there, too.

"Monday, 8/9/1999 - Day 139 - 12.1 miles today, 1686.7 total, average 12.13. It's a pretty morning and there's no excuse not to hike so I'll be headed out soon. I'll be in New Hampshire by Friday if all goes well. Ankle still bothering me. There's a sharp pain when I step a certain way. I'm camped by an old mountain road tonight. It's about dark now and getting pretty cool."

That ankle was going to make Smoky Joe pay dearly for the prize of a lifetime, or make it forfeit it altogether. It just wasn't getting any better.

"Tuesday, 8/10/1999 - Day 140 - 10.7 miles today, 1697.4 total, average 12.12. Tough day today. I'm moving very slowly. Ankle still giving me a lot of trouble. I fell a couple of times today because I lost my balance and couldn't keep any weight on that ankle. It's very frustrating. I hope I don't have to take any time off to let it heal."

But for one brief and shining moment Joe could take his attention off his troubles and place it somewhere else.

"I think I heard and caught a glimpse of a moose this morning. It was close to the trail, about 25 yards, but in very thick brush. I heard

something walking that sounded like a horse and saw something moving. I can't be sure that it was a moose but I don't know what else it could have been."

But the moose wasn't the only surprise of the day for Smoky Joe because just up the road was an institution of higher learning known as Dartmouth College. Now, there at Dartmouth College Smoky Joe would stumble upon a rather strange practice, or at least it was rather strange to that old boy from Jacksonville, Georgia.

But we will have to conclude this part until we continue. Meanwhile, we will leave Joe stranded at Dartmouth College and pick him up again promptly. Maybe he will be safe until then.

Credits: Info of Joe Ward; Info of John David Harrell; Appalachian Trail info; Vermont and New Hampshire info; personal notes; other sources.

Part 38
Smoky Joe Camped At Dartmouth College And Got His Eyes Opened

Smoky Joe Ward of Jacksonville, Ga., was now on the campus of prestigious Dartmouth College, an old Ivy League icon of higher

education. A recent class had an average SAT score of 1470.
Famous graduates and students include US Senator Daniel
Webster, Chief Justice of the United States Salmon P. Chase of
Ohio, Theodor Seuss Geisel (renowned children's author Dr.
Seuss), poet Robert Frost, and Vice President Nelson Rockefeller
of New York. But when Joe found out about certain co-ed activities he
thought it "a strange situation." [Photo and info credit: The Free
Dictionary by Farlex]

Smoky Joe Ward was now up in New Hampshire and not very far
away from getting a "college education" at Dartmouth College. He
almost missed this Ivy League opportunity:

*"Wednesday, 8/11/1999 - Day 141 - 11.7 miles today, 1709.1 total,
average 12.12. I'm still struggling with this sore ankle. If it doesn't get
any worse I think I'll be OK. I'll be in New Hampshire tomorrow.
Dartmouth College in Hanover is right on the Appalachian Trail just
across the state line. I think they let hikers stay on campus but I may
keep going. My slow pace and the two days off in Killington have put
me behind."*

Now, Smoky Joe might not have realized it at the time but he had
just stepped upon the campus of one of the oldest seats of higher
learning in the country - Dartmouth College. In that long time of
existence they had come to be somewhat tolerant of certain viewpoints
and practices. That is not entirely surprising considering they had
students from 50 or so states and 73 foreign countries. They even have
their own college-owned pub. On the other hand, they have two halls or
dorms designated as drug free, alcohol free, and smoke free. So there is
a choice. And that is what it seems life is all about anyway. Of course,
Dartmouth College has made many great contributions to the world we
live in. All computer users certainly owe two Dartmouth professors -
John George Kemeny and Thomas Eugene Kurtz. They developed the
BASIC programming language. Had it not been for those scholars we
would probably still be pecking away on typewriters! And now Smoky
Joe is about to be educated about this garden spot of academia:

*"Thursday, 8/12/1999 - Day 142 - 9.2 miles today, 1718.3 total,
average 12.10. I spent the night in my tent on Dartmouth campus
behind a fraternity house. They let us use the shower, bathroom, etc.
The showers were co-ed. A strange situation."*

Well, before Smoky Joe had absorbed too much learning in these surroundings of erudition he decided it was high time to depart lest he lose sight of another world called Jacksonville, Ga. Also, he wanted to stay focused on more familiar fare as he needed to make it to Maine and Mount Katahdin, the end of his journey. But, even the Dartmouth students could have helped him with this because one of their organizations spends a good bit of their free time keeping up a large portion of the Appalachian Trail and hiking it. In fact, the students have been looking after things quite well for years. Long ago they ran off the herds belonging to farmers who were grazing their cattle on the Dartmouth Green. Now, *"The Green is the physical and emotional center of campus life. Originally used for herding cattle, the Green is now used for anything from snow rugby to ultimate Frisbee to picnics, political rallies, parades, sunbathing, snowshoe races and wood chopping."* Maybe Joe would see some of these folks on The Trail because that was where he was heading:

"Friday, 8/13/1999 - Day 143 - 10.8 miles today, 1729.1 total, average 12.09. Out of town about 8:00 AM. My pack is always heavy with supplies coming out of town and I'm usually climbing up out of a valley. Moose Mountain was my first tough climb in New Hampshire. I only went up 2200 feet but it was pretty steep. I had to carry extra water the last two miles. Got to campsite and was about half way up with my tent when it started raining. I got the tent up quick enough to keep everything dry. It's still raining but I'm nice and dry. It's pleasant lying here listening to the rain hit the tent. I won't be able to cook supper until it stops."

I suppose Joe figured his present position was a world or two away from his stay at Dartmouth College. And he had to contend with the rain out here in nature's wonderland:

"Saturday, 8/14/1999 - Day 144 - 8.8 miles today, 1737.9 total, average 12.06. I got caught in some heavy rain this afternoon about four miles from where I was planning to camp. I got my tent up during a little let-up and decided to stay for the night. It still looks pretty bad. New Hampshire, so far, has been tough and I haven't even got to the White Mountains."

We can see from his entry that Joe has not forgotten that one of those mountains up in that direction boasted world record winds of 231 miles per hour. But Smoky Joe was not turning back now. He had come too far. Right now he would just like some dry weather.

"Sunday, 8/15/1999 - Day 145 - 9.1 miles today, 1747 total, average 12.04. Had light rain most of the day. I stopped at a shelter (fire warden's cabin) on Smarts Mountain about mid-day and thought about staying for the night. I unpacked, ate and rested awhile then decided to go on. I had to put my wet clothes back on. I'm at another shelter now (The Hexacuba). It's 5:30 PM and so far I'm alone."

Joe was glad to see the next town. It had some amenities, although nothing to write home about. At least maybe now he could get dry and comfortable.

"Monday, 8/16/1999 - Day 146 - 14.7 miles today, 1761.7 total, average 12.06. Into Glencliff, New Hampshire, today. I didn't make it in time to go to post office so I'm staying at a hostel right across the street from the post office for $12.00. "Fancy", a girl who hiked the trail in 1996, and her husband run it and live here also. There are mattresses in a loft, an outdoor, warm water, shower and an outdoor privy. We can also use her kitchen and washing machine. There are only three hikers here. One I know pretty well - "Carolina Kid". He is letting me use his New Hampshire maps because he is hiking with someone who has them also. In the morning I start some serious climbing - up to 5000 feet. Mount Moosilauke is the first mountain above tree line in the "Whites". It should be real pretty."

Joe was so right. His photos reveal the almost unbelievable beauty of this area. God has richly blessed us with His creation of grandeur. In so many ways and so many places. Like Gerard Manley Hopkins said, *"The world is charged with the grandeur of God."*

Credits: Info of Joe Ward; Info of John David Harrell; Appalachian Trail info; New Hampshire info; Dartmouth College info; personal notes; other sources.

Part 39

Smoky Joe Sees Fellow Georgian Hiker Thad Childs III

Smoky Joe Ward of Jacksonville, Ga., is now high on one of the mountains of New Hampshire. Joe is cautious about these mountains because they are known for their rugged nature and wind velocity. He is trying not to get blown away by a 231 MPH wind. He also says the rocks here are as tough as those in Pennsylvania. Maybe Maine will be better. He will soon find out. He's only 71 miles away. Joe met hiker Thad Childs III of Gray, Ga., near here. Thad's aunt, Beth Childs Brooks, lives here in Douglas, Ga.

Well, Smoky Joe Ward had gotten a quick education at Dartmouth College and was ready to leave that scene for those of a more pastoral nature. As he roamed these vast rural areas and viewed the great mountain ranges before him Joe was acutely aware that all this majesty was overwhelmingly beautiful - but at the same time fatally dangerous! He had conquered many a peak at this juncture but he did not want to let himself get too confident. It was easy to do and that's when a fellow gets hurt, or worse. Joe was trying to protect himself against such dalliances of the mind. This was no time to be playing dangerous mind games concerning mountain climbing.

"Tuesday, 8/17/1999 - Day 147 - 7.9 miles today, 1769.6 total, average 12.03. Out of Glencliff about 9:30 AM for my climb up the first of the big White Mountains (Mount Moosilauke). It was almost a four-hour climb to the top (almost 5,000 feet). The top was above tree line so there was an awesome view. Shortly after I got on top some bad looking clouds, wind and a little rain came in. It got cool real quick. Everybody talks about how quickly the weather can get bad at high elevations in the White Mountains so I got a little uneasy. I was going to take a long break and enjoy the view but I left pretty quickly. Sometimes, after hiking over 1700 miles I get a little cocky and think I'm tough but mother nature can humble you in a hurry."

Now Smoky Joe was missing that mother of his and I imagine, as my memory is pretty sharp about such things, he was missing Ms. Helen's cooking, too:

"Tuesday, 8/17/1999 - Note to Mrs. Ward - Dear Momma, I haven't been writing you much because I send these notes. They are the same as a letter I suppose. I'm in Glencliff, New Hampshire, where I spent the night in town waiting for the post office to open in the morning. I think about you a lot and look forward to seeing you soon. Love, Joe."

Joe followed the note with a card to his mother and hike coordinator, John David Harrell. He wanted them to know he was about to take yet another big step toward his goal:

"Tuesday, 8/17/1999 - Card - Momma and Johnny, Still waiting for the post office to open. My pack is really going to be heavy again with my heavy clothes and I'll have to add some extra food because it's a long way to Gorham with little in between to resupply. I'm looking forward to the White Mountains. They are supposed to be spectacular. Next food drop - Rangeley, Maine (ETA 9/6). 398 miles to go from Glencliff. Joe."

We find out every day just how small the world is. Here Joe Ward of Jacksonville, Ga., is hiking in the middle of nowhere way up in Yankee Land and look who he runs into:

"Wednesday, 8/18/1999 - Day 148 - 9.1 miles today, 1778.7 total, average 12.01. These beautiful New Hampshire mountains are as tough as I've been hearing. Steep, long climbs and steep rocky down hills. A nine-mile day takes almost as long as a twelve to fifteen-mile day has on easier terrain. One downhill section today on Mount Moosilauke (1.6 miles) took me two hours. I got to the shelter today and was talking to a boy from Macon, Ga. (Childs family is from Gray, Ga., near Macon). It turns out he is Thad Childs, the son of one of Murray's old college buddies. He's hiking south. Only 100.1 miles to Maine."

I called Leo Brooks and his wife, Beth Childs Brooks, here in Douglas, to make sure it was the same family. They assured me that it was Thad Childs III, nephew of Beth, and that he did, indeed, hike the Appalachian Trail. Beth said Thad was now out in Washington State. I suspect that he, like Smoky Joe Ward, is a free spirit and likes to see what is out there to see. Like I said, it is a small world. Who would have thought that a young man from Jacksonville, Ga., would run into a young man from Gray, Ga., on the Appalachian Trail way up in New Hampshire!

"Thursday, 8/19/1999 - Day 149 - 11.4 miles today, 1790.1 total, average 12.01. 370.1 miles left to go."

Joe is eagerly counting down but he still has some of the most picturesque scenes ahead of him:

"Friday, 8/20/1999 - Day 150 - 7.7 miles today, 1797.8 total, average 11.98. I saw some of the prettiest country today that I've seen the whole trip. I hiked over Little Haystack Mountain, Lincoln and Mount Lafayette (over 5000 feet). All above tree line. The 360 degree view was awesome. I'm sure the pictures I took won't do it justice. Most of the campsites in New Hampshire have caretakers who stay at the sites and charge $6.00 to tent. There also is a hut system, mainly for tourists who hike in from roads. Supposedly two thru hikers can stay each night and work for their stay. The normal price is fifty to sixty dollars which includes two meals. I think they also sell leftovers to hikers."

Smoky Joe was finding out in a hurry that this part of the country was no picnic.

"Saturday, 8/21/1999 - Day 151 - 9.7 miles today, 1807.5 total, average 11.97. Strong wind and rain last night. The campsite had wooden tent platforms and I couldn't get my tent fly tight enough so it flapped all night. I stayed dry though. It was raining a little when I took my tent down this morning. It was cloudy and raining all day so there were no views. I stopped at one of the pay huts about 10:00 AM but they didn't have any leftovers. I did get some hot coffee and ate my cereal inside. I added peanuts and M&M's to it. I'm not so sure I like it. "Rhubarb and Jeleb" and a lady from Rhode Island - "Swamp Yankee" - that I just met were there. I got my tent up this afternoon just before it started raining again. I'm close to another hut so maybe I'll get there before the leftovers are gone. At least I'll get coffee. I forgot to mention this early, but New Hampshire rocks are as bad as Pennsylvania. Only 71 miles to Maine."

Maine might just be 71 miles away but this trip was not about over for Smoky Joe Ward of Jacksonville, Ga.!

Thad Childs III
Fellow Georgian Hiker

Thad Was Going South And Joe Was Going North

Thad On The Appalachian Trail
Probably Still Enjoying Outdoors
In Washington State

Credits: Info of Joe Ward; Info of John David Harrell; Appalachian Trail info; New Hampshire info; Thad Childs III info/images of Denise Childs and Beth Childs Brooks; personal notes; other sources.

Part 40

This Mountain Has Some Nasty Weather

At the top of the picture we see Smoky Joe Ward at the weather station at Mt. Washington, New Hampshire. Obviously, the weather isn't too good on Mt. Washington. But Joe hikes on up and over the mountain. He enjoyed beautiful scenery and had the reward of standing by the summit sign that tells us he made it to the top. He's going to take a day's rest and head out for Maine. He'll have problems there, too. [Photographs courtesy of Smoky Joe Ward, Appalachian Trail hiker]

Smoky Joe Ward was having second thoughts about New Hampshire. Now, the scenery was breathtaking and the fresh air was great. And he had met some great people on The Trail. But the climbing and rocks were tough. As tough as he had seen. He hoped Maine would give him a little slack. Only time would tell. Right now he was about to see more moose.

"Sunday, 8/22/1999 - Day 152 - 7.7 miles today, 1815.2 total, average 11.94. I'm doing some short mileage through the White Mountains. There aren't many places to camp so I have to do short days or real long ones which are tough with the terrain and elevation change. Today I hitched a ride to a hostel in Crawford Notch. Room and shower for $14.00. They were full so I camped in the woods close by. I saw two moose this morning. A cow and her calf were only about 15 yards from the trail. They didn't pay me any attention. I took some pictures but it was pretty thick. I don't know how they'll turn out. I've heard that the cows may charge you so I was a little anxious but she kept on feeding. 345 miles to go."

Joe enjoyed the moose and they didn't seem to mind his presence. But the big item loomed not too far off in his field of vision. It was the moment he had been anxiously awaiting. It was the challenge of New Hampshire and perhaps the entire trip. Mount Washington! Hikers talked about it, feared it but smiled if they were able to get over it. It held the world's record for the fastest wind on land - 231 miles per hour! It was also the tallest thing around.

"Monday, 8/23/1999 - Day 153 - 6.4 miles today, 1821.6 total, average 11.90. Another short mileage day, but in addition to the 6.4 miles on the trail I walked another 4 miles on the road from the hostel. I stopped at a little snack bar before getting back on the trail and had breakfast. It's another beautiful day. I hiked over Mount Webster and Mount Jackson (4000 feet). Both are above tree line. The views were awesome. I took several pictures of Mount Washington. I'll go over it tomorrow (6200 feet), the highest peak in New Hampshire. The weather is supposed to be good. Mount Washington is the climb I've been concerned about the whole trip. The weather, supposedly, can change very quickly with high winds, snow and ice even in the summer. It's going to be a relief to get over it. At the same time I'm excited about it. 338.6 miles to go."

As Smoky Joe thought of the big mountain in front of him he thought of home - Jacksonville, Ga. Of similar weather and hunting trips. He looked for good omens. He thought about the mountain being the end of the line, literally, for some of the unfortunate souls of the past. They went up on it but never came down. He tried to dismiss that dismal thought. But all this did not curb his excitement; it just fueled it. Smoky Joe was excited!

"Tuesday, 8/24/1999 - Day 154 - 11.8 miles today, 1833.4 total, average 11.90. It's 4:00 AM. I always wake up early because I go to bed at dark but this morning I'm excited about climbing Mount Washington. The sky is full of stars and it's cool and not too windy. It's like the fall mornings at home that I like to go hunting. I saw a couple of shooting stars and wished for a good end to my trip. It has been a wonderful adventure. The weather was good all day for the climb over Mount Washington. It's cool and sunny. I took a picture of a sign at the base that warned you to turn back if the weather was bad. A lot of people have died over the years on the mountain. I was above tree line all day with nowhere to hide if the weather had gotten bad. 326.8 miles to go."

Now Joe was on his way. There was no turning back now. He might as well enjoy the scenery.

"Wednesday, 8/25/1999 - Day 155 - 7.8 miles today, 1841.2 total, average 11.87. Walking above the tree line in the "Whites" is like walking on the moon. Nothing growing but a few small shrubs here and there. It's just like a huge pile of rocks, but the views of other mountains and valleys make up for it. I took some pictures today to show how rocky it is. It's 37.6 miles to Maine and 319 to Katahdin."

But even now, Joe monitored himself, his mileage and his time closely.

"Thursday, 8/26/1999 - Day 156 - 13.1 miles today, 1854.3 total, average 11.88. The most miles I've done in the "Whites" in one day. It took me from 6:00 AM to 6:30 PM to do it. It's slow going but still very pretty."

Joe cannot believe he is over Mount Washington. The experience has been terrific. His adrenaline is slowing the rate it had maintained for "that big bad mountain." It was time to give thanks and go to town. The giant mountain had been conquered.

"Friday, 8/27/1999 - Day 157 - 8 miles today, 1862.3 total, average 11.86. Into Gorham, New Hampshire for food drop and rest in motel. This will probably be my last good break on the trip. Only 16.5 miles to Maine and 297.9 to Katahdin."

Smoky Joe was elated to get in touch with his contacts at Jacksonville, Ga. He made some changes in his plans upon the advice of his hike coordinator, John David Harrell. It was reassuring to have Johnny studying the situation, too. Two heads are better than one.

"Saturday, 8/28/1999 - Fax - Momma, I'm in Gorham, N.H. Spent the night here in a motel. I felt like I needed a good rest before starting into Maine. It's only 16.5 miles from here to the Maine state line. It's hard to believe that I've finally almost made it. New Hampshire and the White Mountains have been beautiful. The prettiest country I've seen on the whole trip. The hiking has been tough, but the scenery has made up for it. Maine is supposed to be very pretty, too. Johnny probably told you, but it looks now like it will be the end of September when I finish. I want to enjoy these last few weeks and see Maine in the fall with the leaves changing. Maybe it won't be too cold. When I talked to Johnny last night I told him that Rangely, Maine, would be my last food drop (9/6/99). I don't think that he thought that was a good idea and after sleeping on it I think he may be right. So, send me a package to Monson, Maine 04464. ETA 9/15/99. That will definitely be my last one. I miss you and hope you are well. Love, Joe. PS - I'll be here a little while longer so fax me if you can (603) 466-5802. I'll also mail this."

But Joe needed to rest and move on. The problems of Maine were waiting for him.

Credits: Info of Joe Ward; Info of John David Harrell; Appalachian Trail info; New Hampshire info; personal notes; other sources.

Part 41
Maine Greets Smoky Joe
With The Hardest Mile
On The Appalachian Trail

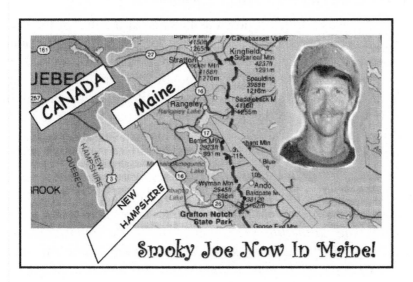

Smoky Joe Now In Maine!

Smoky Joe Ward has now made it to the state of Maine. But he is greeted by "the hardest mile on the Appalachian Trail." It seems to him more like an obstacle course. But things are bound to get better so he presses on hoping that he will see no more miles like the one he has just encountered. [Photo credit: Maine and the Appalachian Trail]

Smoky Joe Ward knew he was probably about to take his last prolonged rest. Or so he thought. He figured he would be too anxious to take another extended breather once he hit the trail for Maine. He was getting close to his goal. One more day in New Hampshire should give him a reservoir of strength for the trek ahead:

"Saturday, 8/28/1999 - Day 158 - 0 miles today, total 1862.3,

average 11.78. Stayed in Gorham, New Hampshire, today and rested. Another day with no hiking."

Joe had made his choice - a heavier load of food going out to save stopping so often. But he knew he was carrying extra weight.

"Sunday, 8/29/1999 - Day 159 - 11.8 miles today, 1874.1 total, average 11.78. Tough hike out of town with eight days food supply. I was going to stop in Andover, before Rangeley, so I wouldn't have to carry so much, but I don't want to lose another day."

Smoky Joe was a little let down as he crossed the line of the final state - Maine. His journey had been a long one but he thought elation at this point might be premature because he still had a long way to go. He had learned much earlier - you don't count your biddies before they hatch. You make one hard step at the time and if you make enough of them you will get there. At this point he knew he had to hang in there. No mishaps, no getting lost, no miscalculations. It was the final leg - and a long one.

"Monday, 8/30/1999 - Day 160 - 9.6 miles today, 1883.7 total, average 11.77. Stayed in a shelter last night by a pretty lake I saw some leeches in the lake while I was filtering water. It was windy and cool this morning. In the fifties. I saw a moose on the opposite side of the lake. I hope the pictures come out. I crossed the Maine state line today. I've been trying to imagine for five months how it would feel to finally get here. It was a good feeling but not as special as I had thought. I guess I'm thinking about the 276.5 miles left."

Smoky Joe was thinking about what was up ahead. He had heard of the "toughest mile on the Appalachian Trail" from other hikers. He anxiously approached this challenge knowing it would take some doing to get through it It was going to be more like an obstacle course than anything else.

"Tuesday, 8/31/1999 - Day 161 - 5.1 miles today, 1888.8 total, average 11.73. I went through the Maloosuc Notch today. It's supposed to be the hardest mile on the Appalachian Trail. It's full of boulders that you have to climb over, under and sometimes through. The openings are so small that you have to take your pack off to get through. It took me two hours to do that mile. 261 miles to go."

As Smoky Joe looked back in the direction of Maloosuc Notch he hoped there would be no more places like that! But pressing on he found it more pleasant.

"Wednesday, 9/1/1999 - Day 162 - 10.4 miles today, 1899.2 total, average 11.72. It's the first day of September and I'm in Maine. The weather is almost perfect. It's cool in the mornings and at night. Still a little warm during the day while hiking, but if I stop for a break I need another shirt on."

Smoky Joe was enjoying his hike now. He was seeing some things, had companions and was able to reach water. It couldn't get much better.

"Thursday, 9/2/1999 - Day 163 - 11.9 miles today, 1911.1 total, average 11.72. It's 1:00 PM and I'm taking a break by Surplus Lake about halfway up Wyman Mountain. I thought about taking a swim but decided to just rest. It's only another four miles to camp. Another ten-mile day but I'm enjoying the pace. The last few days I've been camping with "Corsican", "Mooseburger" and "Old Scot". Ended up doing more than ten miles today. There was no water where I planned to camp. I had to come further down the mountain to Sawyer Notch and a nice stream. I saw a big bull moose this afternoon. He had a rack about three feet wide. I hope I got a good picture. 249.1 miles to go."

But Joe found out, as he had before - you don't take water for granted.

"Friday, 9/3/1999 - Day 164 - 11.4 miles today, 1922.5 total, average 11.72. There's no water at the shelter again. I had to carry extra water a long way. I thought Maine was supposed to have lots of water. I stayed in the shelter tonight instead of the tent. Only one other person here. 237.7 miles to go."

Appropriately, Joe now camped at a place where the day fit the name.

"Saturday, 9/4/1999 - Day 165 - 8.3 miles today, 1930.8 total, average 11.70. Camped on the edge of a pretty lake - Sabbath Day Pond. Supposed to be loons on it but I haven't heard one yet. It's just a little over nine miles to Rangeley for food drop."

Joe was now entering the day the rest of us observe as the Sabbath. Naturally, it would not do to agree on this, either. That just seems to be the nature of man.

"Sunday, 9/5/1999 - Day 166 - 9.4 miles today, 1940.2 total, average 11.68. Heard a wolf last night very early. It was a beautiful sound. I also heard some coyotes. I'm staying in Rangeley at the Farmhouse Inn for $20.00 a night. The blind man who hiked the trail stayed here when he came through and a TV station did a story on him."

Well, it looks like Smoky Joe ran right into Labor Day! This would slow him up a little more.

"Monday, 9/6/1999 - Day 167 - 0 miles today, 1940.2 total, average 11.61. Another "0" day in town. I forgot about the holiday so I have to wait until tomorrow for the post office to open. Not much to do in town and the inn is a mile and a half away so I don't know what I'll do all day. Rest I guess. 220 miles to go."

With the spare time on his hands Joe decided to see what he had in his pack that he could send home. He found something.

"Monday, 9/6/1999 - Card - Momma and Johnny, This is an old post card. I went over Mount Washington a few weeks ago. The small building is one of the huts you pay to stay in. I think I stopped and had some coffee at this one. You can see the trail on the left. Should be in Monson on 9/16/1999. 220 miles to do. Joe."

But Smoky Joe was wanting to see the end of Labor Day. He needed to get on The Trail again. Adventure might be just around the corner.

Credits: Info of Joe Ward; Info of John David Harrell; Appalachian Trail info; New Hampshire and Maine info; personal notes; other sources.

Part 42

Still Some Obstacles – Including A Law Enforcement Officer

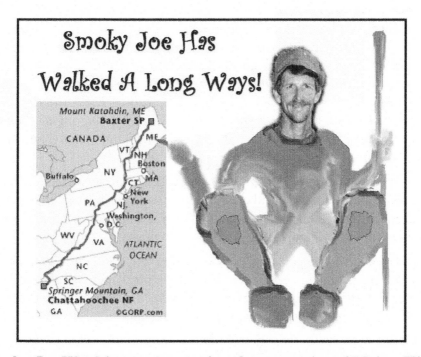

Smoky Joe Ward is now conquering the mountains of Maine. His boots are getting a little worn but his spirits are high. He is not far from his goal of finishing his journey. But he keeps running into unexpected situations. Like being stopped by a law enforcement officer. The Trail is full of surprises and he looks forward to the next ones. Or, so he thinks.

Smoky Joe Ward woke up the next morning not knowing he would be taking up time with the questions of a Maine law enforcement officer. Or meeting two people who would be attracting the attention of this law enforcement officer.

"Tuesday, 9/7/1999 - Day 168 - 1.8 miles today, 1942 total, average

11.55. Didn't get out of Rangeley early enough today to make it over the Saddleback Mountains, which are supposed to be pretty tough. I stopped at the first shelter out of town. It's supposed to rain the next few days, so I'm trying to stop at shelters. I got a ride from the Farmhouse Inn back to the trail with a young couple (Doug and Chris) who are traveling around the country. They're living in their van and looking for work along the way. They had recently been working on a horse farm somewhere. They were nice people, but pretty rough looking. They had tattoos, long hair, etc. Their van was pretty ragged also. On the way back to the trail a deputy sheriff stopped us and checked Doug out pretty good. I was afraid I might get to stay in Rangeley a little longer, but he let us go. They were very interested in the trail and walked with me a little ways. The owners of the Farmhouse Inn were good people. I ate with them one night. Rick and Meg Godaire, Farmhouse Inn, PO Box 165, Route 4, Rangeley, Maine 04970. Phone 207-864-5805."

Joe realized the long stopover had caused him to wax long (and in detail) about the new world around him. But he also knew his energies had to be redirected to The Trail again. Talking and describing would not get him to Mount Katahdin. He had to push on.

"Johnny's going to get tired of typing the notes for this day. I've had so much time at the shelter that I'm getting longwinded. I've had a good rest since Sunday afternoon. Two days in Rangeley and a short hike today. I'm ready for the last push to Katahdin."

But the resolve was there. Smoky Joe started picking 'em up and putting 'em down. He eyed the great mountains in front of him and despite the rain, he left those high hills of Maine behind him. He was on his way.

"Wednesday, 9/8/1999 - Day 169 - 8.9 miles today, 1950.9 total, average 11.54. Hard rain last night. It's good to be in a shelter. Overcast and threatening to rain all day, so I'm in another shelter tonight. I went over some of the last few major climbs today - Saddleback and The Horn, but I couldn't see much because of the clouds."

Joe is lining up mountains now much the same as a shopper makes out a shopping list. And he is anticipating checking them off as he clears them. His schedule of time and distance is ever on his mind. He knows that the discipline of the trail matters all. There are no excuses - just executions. He must keep executing. He must keep on the schedule.

"Thursday, 9/9/1999 - Day 170 - 8 miles today, 1958.0 total, average 11.52. Still getting cloudy weather from the hurricane on the coast. Only sprinkles so far today. I'm tenting tonight because I sleep better than in a shelter. I'll probably have to pack a wet tent in the morning. Only a few big mountains left before I get into some easier terrain - Spaulding, Sugarloaf, and Crocker mountains. I'll do those tomorrow. Bigelow Mountain should be the last one for a while. I'm looking forward to doing more miles each day. If I had stayed on my original schedule I'd only have ten days left. 201.3 miles left."

In spite of his enthusiasm, the physical dampness was upon him again and Smoky Joe decided it was time for another break. In a little bit there would be no time or provisions for relaxing in civilized surroundings. Just wilderness.

"Friday, 9/10/1999 - Day 171 - 13.5 miles today, 1972.4 total, average 11.53. Rained all day. Hitched a ride into Stratton for the night. $20.00 for a private room. 187.8 miles left."

But through all the rain, focusing on the schedule, and the awareness of "the wilderness" before him, Joe felt good. His mind was taking it all in and he felt he was up to doing this last memorable leg of his journey in Maine. Little did he know that Canada was not far from him.

"Saturday, 9/11/1999 - Day 172 - 8 miles today, 1980.4 total, average 11.51. Camped on Bigelow Mountain. It's the last major climb I'll have until I get to Katahdin. It's a very pretty mountain. I didn't realize how close I am to the Canadian border. Only 20 or 30 miles I think. There are some other campers here and most of them are speaking French. I almost can't believe it, but I may be able to finish in two weeks."

After bidding 'Adieu' to his French compeers, Smoky Joe headed out, not knowing that he would run right in on a group with eating on their minds. And he was happy to be much obliged for their warm invitation which included a great helping of those tasty rations.

"Sunday, 9/12/1999 - Day 173 - 14.6 miles today, 1995 total, average 11.53. Hiked down off Bigelow Mountain this morning leaving the toughest portion of the trail behind me. Maybe I'll make some good time now, unless it's so pretty that I want to go slow. Just after getting down off the mountain, the trail crossed a road. The Maine Appalachian Trail Club was having a cookout for thru hikers there. I ate way too much because I still had to hike six miles, but it was good. I crossed another paved road after that and it had 2000 miles written in big yellow print right in the middle of the road. By my math I've been only 1995 miles, but that's close enough. I had to take my boots off to wade a stream today. I may be seeing a lot of that. I'm camped by a pretty lake tonight."

Now, folks, Smoky Joe Ward had a way of being profoundly prophetic. Yes, he was going to see lots of "that" and a whole bunch more before this little trip was over.

Credits: Info of Joe Ward; Info of John David Harrell; Appalachian Trail info; New Hampshire and Maine info; personal notes; other sources.

Part 43
Traitor Benedict Arnold Might Have Placed A Curse On This Wilderness

Smoky Joe Ward had reached Monson, Maine. He was enjoying the great scenery in the last state of his Appalachian Trail hike. But he was eager to complete his journey. But things like rain and getting lost would get in his way. And it wasn't such a good idea to get lost in Maine's One Hundred Mile Wilderness. Maybe traitor Benedict Arnold had put a curse on the trail when he came through more than 200 years before. [Photo credit: Town of Monson, Maine]

Smoky Joe Ward couldn't believe he would soon be retracing the steps of the great American Benedict Arnold who went from that status to traitor of his country. Benedict was a brave man and contributed greatly to the American cause before being siphoned off by the moneyed British and a pretty woman. Benedict had suffered a lot for his American efforts and had a bum leg to show for it. The leg was injured in battle and then a horse fell on it so Arnold was not in a good mood about his physical well-being, either. Somewhat infuriated by younger officers being promoted above him and other disagreements with the colonial government he gradually succumbed to the wooing of the enemy, the British. All in all it was a sad chapter for our country and for Benedict Arnold. After his defection no one, American or British, trusted him.

"Monday,   9/13/1999 - Day 174 - 10 miles today, 2005 total, average 11.52. It's noon and I'm taking a break. I got a lazy start this morning (9:00 AM). I'm only doing ten miles today because tomorrow I cross the Kennebec River. There's no bridge but the Maine Appalachian Trail Club has a canoe there from 9 to 11 AM to take people across. I'll camp about three miles south of there so I can be there by 9:00 AM tomorrow. Since the heavy rain last Friday the weather has been perfect. Cool mornings and nights with sunny days. The trail has been almost flat for the last fifteen miles. I'm walking by a lot of pretty lakes. There are still a lot of rocks, roots and boggy places to slow me down. I've been on the Arnold Trail today. During the Revolutionary War Benedict Arnold came through here with about 1000 men headed to Quebec to fight the British. His army bogged down in the swamps and never made it to Canada on time. It turns out that what I thought were wolves howling were loons. They can make several different sounds and it's amazing how much one sounds like a wolf. I'm camped on another lake. 155.2 miles to go."

Smoky Joe seems to be enjoying his trek through Maine at this point. Obviously those folks up there in the woods were expecting hikers because they were ready with their boats to ferry them across the streams.

"Tuesday, 9/14/1999 - Day 175 - 9.7 miles today, 2014.7 total, average 11.51. Made it to the Kennebec River just before 9:00 AM and the man was on the other side with the canoe. He came right over to get me. The river was about 75 yards wide and looked pretty swift but not deep. Some people have waded across but I didn't want to chance slipping and getting everything wet. I got some pictures of the river and the canoe. I went into Caratunk (.25 mile off trail) to get a few things. There was only a small general store with a post office inside. I'm hiking less and eating more now so I may gain some of my weight back before I get home. I've made a rough schedule of my days for the rest of the trip and it looks like I'll finish on September 27. Only 13 days from now. 145.5 miles to go."

Smoky Joe was now dreaming of the beautiful country he was hiking and the soon-to-be end of a great adventure.

"Wednesday, 9/15/1999 - Day 176 - 13.1 miles today, 2027.8 total, average 11.52. I'm camped by another lake, listening to the loons. It's good to be around lakes and streams again. Everything is still green. I thought I'd be seeing some leaves changing by now. There's a little yellow on birch trees but that's about it. I'm going to try and make it into Monson tomorrow."

With the beautiful scenery Smoky Joe was also eagerly wanting to see Monson because at that town there would be a chance for good food and getting out a postcard or two.

"Thursday, 9/16/1999 - Day 177 - 14.6 miles today, 2042.4 total, average 11.53. It started raining during the night so I had to pack up in the rain this morning. It rained on me most of the day into Monson but I enjoyed the hike. I'm staying at Shaw's boarding house. Twenty-five dollars a night for a private room and shared bath. Good home-cooked family style food and good people. 117.8 miles to go."

Smoky Joe was staying in touch with reality up in the Maine woods but was also staying in touch with home and friends at Jacksonville, Ga. He hoped to see them soon.

"Friday, 9/17/1999 - Day 178 - 0 miles today, 2042.4 total, average 11.47. It's still raining so I'm going to stay another day. Still getting bad weather from Hurricane "Floyd" but it's supposed to clear up tomorrow. Had a good talk with Johnny this morning. Looks like I'll be flying home on the thirtieth (30th)."

Monson, Maine, was not a metropolis but it surely was good to be there. It was also good to be out of the wilderness for a spell.

"Friday, 9/17/1999 Card - Momma and Johnny, I'm in Monson, Maine, waiting this storm out. This is a postcard of the man who carried me across the Kennebec River. Looks like I'm all set to fly home on the 30th. Looking forward to seeing you. Joe."

Another card went out the next day, too. Smoky Joe had seen a lot of rain and it was getting in the way of his progress.

"Saturday, 9/18/1999 - Momma and Johnny, I'm still in Monson. The rain has stopped but there are several flooded creeks north of here

that I can't cross. I plan to leave this afternoon, but I may not get far. Hopefully, I can get back on schedule, but if I have a problem I'll try to get word to you some way. Joe."

Funny that Smoky Joe was talking about getting back on schedule because he was not about to get back on schedule right now. In fact, he was on his way to getting lost. And no less, in the Maine One Hundred Mile Wilderness. And we will see how Joe managed that - soon.

Credits: Info of Joe Ward; Info of John David Harrell; Appalachian Trail info; Maine info; personal notes; other sources.

Part 44

Smoky Joe Waiting For A Boat – The Trail Here Was Wet

Smoky Joe Ward poses at one of the falls on the Little Wilson stream in Maine. The rains came and the creeks, rivers and lakes became major challenges. But Smoky Joe meant to get across those places some way or the other. He had to take some detours and sometimes those detours got him lost. Finding his way out of the 100 Mile Wilderness became "interesting."

Well, you never know what you might be getting into when you take a detour. Detours can be tricky things. And Smoky Joe Ward was about to find this out.

"Saturday, 9/18/1999 - Day 179 - 6.3 miles today, 2048.7 total, average 11.44. The rain has stopped and it's a pretty, sunny day, but it rained an awful lot and many streams are flooded along the trail. I only made it to the first shelter today and started seeing people coming back saying there was a stream ahead that couldn't be crossed. (It was Little Wilson.) After deciding to stay here, hoping the water would be down

by tomorrow, some south bounders came by and told me how to get around the flooded area. I'll have to get off the trail and do a short road walk. It's an old logging road with a bridge. Hopefully I'll make some miles tomorrow."

Smoky Joe was about to make some miles for sure - but in the wrong direction. He not only took one detour but some folks back there in the Maine wilderness gave him additional directions that would lead him farther astray. But Joe didn't label all this "frustrating." He merely said it was "interesting." I bet it was.

"Sunday, 9/19/1999 - Day 180 - 16.1 miles today, 2064.8 total, average 11.47. My second day in the "100 Mile Wilderness" was an interesting one. I took the logging road detour around Little Wilson and Big Wilson streams but the road that I had been told to take back to the trail would leave me on the south side of Long Pond stream which was also flooded. I talked with some men at a hunting camp and they told me about a bridge over Long Pond stream and a trail that would lead back to the Appalachian Trail. I either got on the wrong trail or they gave me some bad information because the trail ran out before hitting the Appalachian Trail. Fortunately I had the maps and a compass and was able to find my way up Barren Mountain and get back on the Appalachian Trail. Those white blazes looked pretty good when I found them."

If you've never been lost you don't know the relief Joe felt. Being lost in a swamp or wilderness is no good feeling. Joe was glad to be back where he was supposed to be. Even if the going was a little tough.

"Monday, 9/20/1999 - Day 181 - 11.3 miles today, 2076.1 total, average 11.47. It was a tough hike over the Chairback Range today. It wasn't very steep but it had a lot of short, rocky up-and-downs. I had to wade the west branch of the Pleasant River. It was about forty yards across and about thigh deep. I'm camped on the north side. 84.1 miles to go."

There is one thing Smoky Joe never got used to and it seemed it was around a good bit - rain. He had lived with the rain from the beginning of his trip right on up until now. It wasn't exactly the rain Joe disliked. It was the mess it caused.

"Tuesday, 9/21/1999 - Day 182 - 12.7 miles today, 2088.8 total,

average 11.47. It started raining about daylight so I had a bad start today. I had to pack a wet tent. That has been one of my least favorite things to do on this trip. That and putting up a tent in the rain. I don't mind hiking in the rain. It's the starting and stopping that's tough. It rained on me all day, but I'm in the shelter now and I'm warm and dry. I went over the last major climb between here and Katahdin today. This was White Cap Mountain. It should be easy going now unless the mud is knee-deep. I should be in Baxter State Park in five days. If the weather permits I'll climb Katahdin the next day (9/27/1999)."

Joe now had his remaining trail days numbered within the limits of a week or less. Looking back at his months on The Trail made him realize that he was now near his destination. It was a good feeling.

"Wednesday, 9/22/1999 - Day 183 - 11.7 miles today, 2100.5 total, average 11.47. It was still raining this morning. I hiked in the rain most of the day. I'm staying in another packed shelter tonight. Hopefully it will clear up and I can get back in my tent for the last few nights. I enjoy it much more. I had to wade the east branch of the Pleasant River today. It wasn't very wide but it was mid-thigh deep and very swift. I had to make a couple of tries before I found a spot I could cross. The trail is still very wet and muddy. I've had wet feet for two days now but at least it's not cold. 59.7 miles to go."

The final things are now coming together for Smoky Joe Ward. Today he looks out across the wild blue yonder and sees the goal of his whole journey - Mount Katahdin! He is a happy hiker.

"Thursday, 9/23/1999 - Day 184 - 14.4 miles today, 2114.9 total, average 11.49. It finally cleared up today. We're supposed to have good weather for a few days. Hopefully I'll have a good day to climb Mt. Katahdin on the 27th. I had my first view of Mt. Katahdin today. I could see it very clearly across a lake and a pine forest. The summit was in the clouds and it was beautiful. I was afraid that when I saw it I'd be disappointed, but I was very impressed. It looks like the 100 Mile Wilderness isn't so wild after all. I'm sleeping in a bed tonight. It's a hunting and fishing camp called White House Landing. To get here I had to walk a mile down a logging road, then take a trail through the woods to Pemadumcook Lake. At the lake you blow an air horn and someone comes across in a boat to get you. A young man and his wife (Bill and Linda) run it. There is no electricity. They have gas lanterns, a

wood stove and an outhouse. There is hot running water so I had a shower. I had a hamburger and homemade apple cake with cool whip for supper. The apples came off their trees. We'll have pancakes for breakfast and then Bill will take me back across the lake. Bill's dad, "Poopa Jack," hiked the trail this year and has already finished. I met him in Virginia. I'm up at 4:00 AM this morning and excited about finishing my trip. There's a full moon over the lake."

In the beauty of it all Smoky Joe Ward was taking in and cherishing what he knew was a historic journey in his life. He had never done it before and might never do it again. He had experienced a high point in his life - in fact, many high points - along those lofty mountain peaks of the Appalachian Trail. But he was not through. Mount Katahdin loomed in its majesty before him. In just a little while it was going to be man against mountain. But Joe felt up to it. He was about to climb Mt. Katahdin in Maine and end an exciting journey that had started in Georgia.

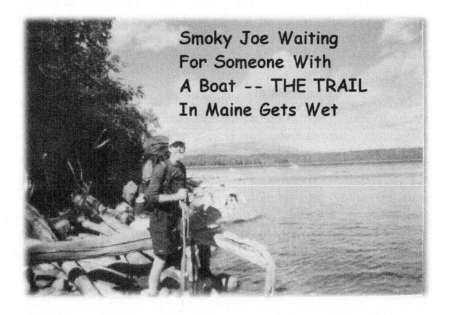

Smoky Joe Waiting
For Someone With
A Boat -- THE TRAIL
In Maine Gets Wet

Credits: Info of Joe Ward; Info of John David Harrell; Appalachian Trail info; Maine info; personal notes; other sources.

Part 45

Victory! End Of The Appalachian Trail – It Was Over!

Smoky Joe Ward of Jacksonville, Ga., is standing on the top of Mount Katahdin in Maine. A journey of 2,160 miles is complete. He has reached his goal. He has hiked the Appalachian Trail. It has been a grand experience and sometimes a trying ordeal. But all that is behind. History. It is over.

Smoky Joe Ward was closing in on Mount Katahdin like a wild game hunter would stalk his quarry. His mind was on it. He looked that way often. There it was. Majestic. Foreboding. Awesome. Beautiful. Definitely a challenge. Not much use trying to sleep with the prize of over 2,000 miles within eyeshot. The adrenaline was trying to pump. Smoky Joe was trying to keep his cool. But it was hard. He had come so far. And now he was about to deliver the coup de grace. Joe smiled. The wet clothes and tents and sore feet and no water at times had been worth it. Katahdin was worth the trip. It was worth the wait. Now there it was. In a way, it all seemed like a dream. Like the mountain would disappear as the clouds hovering around it. But Joe looked again. It was not disappearing. It was there. Permanently.

"Friday, 9/24/1999 - Day 185 - 12.8 miles today, 2127.7 total, average 11.50. I had breakfast and got back across the lake about 8:30 AM. I had another view of Katahdin today. It was perfect weather this morning with about 50 degree temperature and sunshine. I'm in my tent about thirty feet from the bank of Pollywog stream. It's a nice camp and I'm alone."

Joe felt the silence and reverence of the loneliness. He was alone and glad of it. Only The Almighty was sharing this moment with him. It was a good moment.

For some reason Smoky Joe's mind began to backtrack and review, as a procession, those individuals who at one time or another crossed his path on The Trail:

"Saturday, 9/25/1999 - Day 186 - 13.9 miles today, 2141.6 total, average 11.51. These are some trail names of some of the people I've hiked with recently: T Roy (Minnesota), Caboose, Songbird (Maine), Wild Flower (New York City),Chile (?),Wandering Toast (Miami), Carolina Kid (North Carolina), Heavy (North Carolina), Gray Man (South Carolina), Captain (?), Circuit Rider (?), Ulysses (?), Fenrir (Minnesota)."

But try as he may at putting these things on the register of his brain, one thing loomed above all - Katahdin! Every chance Joe got he would gaze into the distance to pick up the indelible image of that great bulk. Yes, there it was. Still there.

"It rained last night but cleared up today. I had another view of

Katahdin today. Tomorrow will be my last real day of hiking. It's only about eight miles to Baxter State Park. There's four miles left in the wilderness. I'll camp in the park and climb Katahdin Monday."

Joe couldn't believe he was saying that. But he was and it was difficult to keep from being ecstatically excited.

"Sunday, 9/26/1999 - Day 187 - 11 miles today, 2152.6 total, average 11.51. I got an early start this morning. I was excited about getting to Baxter. I got to the store at Abol Bridge, the end of the wilderness, about 9:30 this morning. I had some coffee, doughnuts and milk. I bought about three days' food supply just in case I had to wait out bad weather. The weather is supposed to be good tomorrow but you never know. As I write this I'm looking across Daicey Pond at Katahdin. It's a beautiful day with blue sky and no clouds. I hope to start early in the morning. Up Katahdin and back down is about 13 miles. Katahdin is supposed to be a tough climb. It really hasn't hit me yet that it will be all over tomorrow."

Now came the day - Monday. And Joe was ready.

"Monday, 9/27/1999 - Day 188 - 7.6 miles today, 2160.2 total, average 11.49. The weather today is supposed to be sunny. Lows will be in the 30s and highs in the 60s with a chance of patchy frost. It's perfect! I didn't sleep well last night because I was too excited. I awoke several times and thought about starting out in the dark with my head light. I got up at 5:00 AM and took the tent down. I packed in the dark and started hiking about 6:00 AM. It was just getting light. I hiked about 2.5 miles from Daicey Pond Campground to Katahdin Stream Campground at the base of Katahdin. Here I left my big pack and put on a day pack with some extra clothes, water, cheese, crackers and Snickers. It was a little over 5 miles from there to the summit. It took me a little over three hours. I reached the top at 10:40 AM on a beautiful sunny morning. Several people I had hiked with recently, but didn't know too well, were already on top. These were Dick Christian, Second Wind, Captain, Rick Rock, The Great Huebeeny, Mo and her mom."

It was a little more company and hoopla than Joe had anticipated.

"A group that had done the trail and summited 20 years ago to the day arrived later. One of the men had written a book on the trail, "As Far As The Eye Can See," and was doing an article, "Story Of This

Reunion Trip." He was also interviewing this year's through hikers for a side bar to the story. A photographer was with him taking pictures. The summit was starting to get crowded and taking some of the enjoyment out of it for me, so I didn't stick around for my interview. The author had some connection with the National Geographic Traveler Magazine."

It was about to be over.

"After climbing down I hitched a ride into Millinocket to the Appalachian Trail lodge where I'll rest for a couple of days. I'll be flying out of Bangor on the thirtieth to Atlanta where I'll meet Bob Walker and Johnny Harrell for the drive home to Jacksonville, Ga."

It was over.

Credits: Info of Joe Ward; Info of John David Harrell; Appalachian Trail info; Maine info; personal notes; other sources.

Also from Julian Anderson Williams
from ThomasMax Publishing

We Enjoyed Alaska -- But Russell Just About Killed Us!

Julian, a native of Jacksonville, GA, started noticing the impact of Georgia on Alaska, including the personalities migrating to the Great Land. Finding an unusual grave (the person was only 42 years of age) near the Ocmulgee River Swamp at China Hill (near Jacksonville), Julian's curiosity got the best of him when he signed on for a 31-day tour, including Alaska. His main objective was to learn more about the person buried in that grave, Chief Justice of the Supreme Court of Alaska, George F. Boney. Williams also found other colorful folks who left indelible marks and lasting significant contributions for Alaska. But the grand experience of Alaska, along with the laughter, was tempered by the vinegar and spice of a reluctant fellow traveler, Russell Collins, who contended that all information, history and progress of Alaska were subject to his interpretation. To this end, he "explained" the way it was while at the same time working tirelessly to get away from the tour group by trying to catch the next plane home to Georgia. $13.95.

Also from ThomasMax by South Georgia Authors

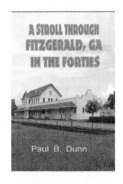

A Stroll Through Fitzgerald, GA, In The Forties by Paul B. Dunn, $14.95. Take an imaginary stroll through the streets of Fitzgerald, Georgia, in the post-World War II era. The walk may be imaginary, but the streets, the businesses, the people -- and the atmosphere of a simpler era -- are all very real.

Lightning Slinger of Andersonville by Paul B. Dunn, $14.95. The story of Teddie O'Dunn, a telegrapher-depot agent who began his career on the railroad in Andersonville, then moved to Fitzgerald, a colony city comprised of Yankees and southerners. Warned to stay away from Yankee girls in Fitzgerald, Teddie was "lightning struck" by the granddaughter of a cavalryman in General Sherman's Army. $14.95. A companion book about Teddie's wife, *Tremble Chin*, is also available by Dunn for $14.95.

Walk With Me by J.D. Lankford, $11.95. Take a walk with Broxton, Georgia's J.D. Lankford through the hard times of the Great Depression, through his work in the CCC and through his Army career, including his time as a Prisoner of War in Nazi Germany. After returning home and getting married, he re-enlisted and was dispatched to Korea, where he earned 5 bronze stars to go with the 4 he had earned in World War II. Some anecdotes are amusing, but many more are horrific and he warns the reader who walks with him: "Don't get involved. You won't like it."

ThomasMax books are available almost everywhere books are sold and through internet sellers such as Amazon.com. If your favorite bookstore doesn't have the book you want in stock, ask the store to order it for you. You may also purchase all ThomasMax titles from www.thomasmax.com via PayPal.

CPSIA information can be obtained at www.ICGtesting.com
Printed in the USA
BVOW08s2113201215

430694BV00001BA/86/P